SOCIAL INTERACTION AND THE DEVELOPMENT OF LANGUAGE AND COGNITION

Social Interaction and the Development of Language and Cognition

Alison F. Garton
*Health Department of
Western Australia*

 LAWRENCE ERLBAUM ASSOCIATES, PUBLISHERS
Hove (UK)   Hillsdale (USA)

Copyright © 1992 by Lawrence Erlbaum Associates Ltd.

Lawrence Erlbaum Associates Ltd., Publishers
27 Palmeira Mansions
Church Road
Hove
East Sussex, BN3 2FA
U.K.

British Library Cataloguing in Publication Data

Garton, Alison F., *1952–*
   Social interaction and the development of language and cognition. –
   (Essays in developmental psychology. ISSN 0959-3977)
   I. Title II. Series
   155

   ISBN 0-86377-227-7 (Hbk)

Printed and bound by Redwood Press Ltd., Melksham, Wilts.

Contents

Acknowledgements

I would like to thank Sue Chambers and Ron Gold for reading portions of an earlier draft of this book, and Sue Leekam and Chris Pratt for reading the entire first draft. I also appreciate the immense efforts of the anonymous reviewers of the book in manuscript form. Their comments and criticisms have helped enormously, as well as their suggestions for the inclusion of additional material in places. Final responsibility for inclusions, exclusions, opinions and interpretations, as usual, rests with the author.

Acknowledgement is given for permission to use the following copyright figures: to the Pergamon Press for Figure 6.3 from W. Doise and G. Mugny (1984) The Social Development of the Intellect; to the Academic Press for Figure 1 from M. Azmitia and M. Perlmutter (1989) Social influences on children's cognition: State of the art and future directions, in H. Reese (Ed.), Advances in Child Development and Behavior, Vol. 22; and to The Society for Research in Child Development for Figure 1 from J.V. Wertsch, G.D. McNamee, J.B. McLane, and N.A. Budwig, (1980), The adult–child dyad as a problem-solving system. *Child Development, 51,* 1215-1221.

CHAPTER ONE

Social Interaction and Development

This book explores an important research question in contemporary developmental psychology. The question to be considered is:

How does social interaction influence the development and growth of knowledge, in particular, cognitive and linguistic knowledge?

In answering this question, what will emerge will be an extensive coverage of the arguments and issues, the pros and cons of different perspectives and the opportunity to contemplate some fundamental theoretical and empirical research in developmental psychology. Therefore, in this introductory chapter, I intend to convince the reader of the validity of the underlying assumptions or presuppositions which then lay the basis for the subsequent discussions of research.

Traditionally (with some notable exceptions, as shall be discussed below), there tends to be both a conceptual and a research separation of cognitive and linguistic development, both developments being driven by different conceptualisations of the developing child advocated by different theoreticians. I believe this characterisation is erroneous as I shall argue there are many overlapping issues in both the study of language development and the study of cognitive development. Further, by adopting and emphasising the impact the child's interaction with the social world can have on the development of her knowledge and understanding of the world, various theoretical and empirical threads can be drawn together. The predominant emphasis is going to be given in this volume to the role that social interaction can play in *encouraging, facilitating* or *causing* cognitive and linguistic growth.

BASES OF KNOWLEDGE

Broadly speaking, there are two sources of knowledge: knowledge is biologically determined or it derives from social origins. This dichotomy is often characterised as the "nature/nurture" debate whereby the development of knowledge is regarded as stemming either from innate pre-set capacities within the child or, alternatively, experience regulates the development of the child's mind through the provision of stimulation for knowledge to grow. Vigorous arguments have raged for centuries over the correctness of these opposing views with all manner of evidence being brought to bear. Both poles in the debate have been represented as theoretical positions in the study of the development of language and of cognition. Each, too, has strongly influenced research either along a particular theme or at a particular time. Today it is common for a middle position to be adopted, whereby the child is regarded as possessing innate predispositions which manifest themselves via interaction with the environment. Psychobiological research has convinced us of the existence of plastic, malleable neural networks which change and develop in relation to environmental stimulation. In the case of the growth of cognitive and linguistic knowledge, it is widely believed that innate in-built mechanisms predispose the child to perceive and to organise her world in culturally acceptable ways. Broadly, genes act flexibly to determine the limit and the range of the reactions possible to environmental stimulation. The genetic endowment delimits the potential courses of action and reaction to the environment in which the child is growing up. By the same token, the nature of the environment can permit or inhibit the expression of the potential reactivity. There is thus a close and sensitive interplay between the child's genetic determinants and the quality and the quantity of the environmental stimuli encountered.

So far, I have ignored the fact that the emphasis in innate views of development tends to be on the *product* of that development, while emphasis on the social and cultural origins of knowledge tends to be on the *process* of development. By this I mean that when assuming an innate component to development, researchers, both empiricists and theoreticians, tend to focus on the end result, the goal to which the child is striving. The child is predisposed towards some end point, some level (usually) higher than that which exists now. Examples would include the development of walking and of adult grammatical competence. By contrast, focus on the social and/or cultural origins of cognitive and linguistic knowledge results in an examination of the environmental or contextual conditions that facilitate the process of development. Examples of culturally or socially determined knowledge include the development of sex roles and morality. This volume is making the assumption that the correct focus for developmental psychology is on the processes of growth and development; thus, it follows that the perspective is going to be on the social and cultural conditions that facilitate cognitive and linguistic development.

It should now be clear that the book is going to examine in depth the relation between social interaction, language and cognition in the developing child. For most of the book, language is regarded as communication. Typically language acquisition studies that incorporate social factors are concerned with the nature of the communicative process between the child and another person, rather than on structural and grammatical developments as such. Early language studies stressed the acquisition by the child of grammar, or language structure. The shift in emphasis from language studies conducted in the 1960s with their focus on structural linguistic developments to later communication studies with greater attention to semantics and pragmatics will be illustrated in the research discussed in Chapter 2. A chronological perspective will highlight this change in emphasis.

Further, cognitive development is regarded as an active process, requiring social facilitation for optimum growth. However, within this framework will be included Vygotsky's view that language is a necessary component in cognitive development. Specifically, language is regarded as a representational system, a system that mediates in cognitive development. Language in a Vygotskian framework is fundamental to all knowledge, both as an interpersonal, communicative system and as a cognitive, representational system permitting development. It will be considered in this manner in this book.

This distinction between the function of language as communication and of cognition as representation can be seen in the opposing theoretical perspectives offered by Piaget and Vygotsky. These perspectives can be compared and contrasted by viewing the role of language as a representational system. Piaget regarded language as representation. He argued for the primacy of thought with language only becoming necessary as thought became more abstract, requiring mental representation to permit efficiency and to enable further cognitive development. Vygotsky (e.g. 1962, 1986), on the other hand, stated that verbal communication was only possible *because* of representation. That is, linguistic representation only emerges because of the demands of human communication. Thinking is considered to be an activity developing in parallel with speech, but maintained in the social context. From prelinguistic thought, interpersonal interaction permitted the expression via speech of the representation of social and cultural attitudes. These could be transferred, along with the social responsibility for their interpretation and implementation, from one participant to another. This fusion of language and thought has been dubbed "emergent interactionism" (Wertsch, 1985a; Kohlberg & Wertsch, 1987). Emergent interactionism forms the basis for the important notion of the transfer of responsibility as being a fundamental function of social interaction, provided one participant has the knowledge and the other does not have the knowledge but requires or can utilise it.

These two polarised positions on the relation between linguistic and cognitive development have informed to a greater or lesser extent contemporary research that has examined how social influences impinge on the growth of knowledge. By and large, the two domains of cognitive development and language development have retained separate identities with consequently different research programmes. Attempts have been made to bridge the gap, and it is my intention to draw out some commonalities and to specify the relation between social interaction, language (as communication) and cognition (as representation). A case has previously been made (Garton & Pratt, 1989) for social interaction and the development of literacy skills (both spoken and written language) to be regarded as integrated. A stronger formulation should emerge here as a result of considering a broader range of research studies, a more diverse sample of theoretical models and by including pertinent research examining the possible facilitatory role of social interaction in processes of development.

THEORIES OF DEVELOPMENT

Starting from the premise that we are interested in describing and explaining the processes of human development, there are possibly four important theorists who have informed research studies over the past three decades. Citations to at least one of the four can be found in virtually every paper and book on human psychological development. The four are Jean Piaget, Lev Vygotsky, Noam Chomsky and Jerome Bruner. All, except Chomsky, have been concerned with *how* development occurs, what processes promote development and what facilitates development. Piaget, Bruner and Vygotsky are linked to theories stressing that development consists of *qualitative* changes in children's knowledge, changes in how they think or talk. Further, each has been concerned with how social interaction, or social influences, can permit the development of cognition and language. Piaget and Vygotsky each also contributed to a more integrated position concerned with the development of both thought and language (see Piaget, 1926; Vygotsky, 1962, 1986). While Chomsky himself was more concerned with the development of a universal structural grammar for language, his ideas, and the criticisms of his ideas, led to the study of language development in a social, interactional, context. Although his theoretical formulations have not in themsélves provided the bases for such research, his relative neglect of the development of language, and in particular the social development of language, has provoked an enormous research body over the years.

These four theoretical positions therefore inform to a greater or lesser extent the rest of this volume. I will take each of the positions in turn and illustrate firstly how each has been interpreted to provide a theoretical basis for specific research studies. The relative contribution of each to the study of the social facilitation of cognitive and/or linguistic development will be outlined, as will broad commonalities between different perspectives. What follows is a brief description of each theory, extracting and elaborating on only those aspects necessary for the subsequent chapters. Historically, Vygotsky and Piaget predate Bruner and Chomsky but here I will discuss them in the order resulting from the organisation of the book.

Chomsky's Theory

Chomsky's theory of language development which lays the foundation for the research discussed in Chapter 2, evolved from his descriptions of the universal structural properties of language (see, for example, Chomsky, 1957, 1965). His primary aim was to elucidate a theory of the structure of language that could and would account for the production of all, and only, grammatical sentences by native speakers of a language. Based on the production of language, he sought to demonstrate a speaker's competence with language, in particular its grammar. This grammar would at best be universal, able to describe and explain the grammatical sentences uttered by all those who used language. It would also be able to predict agrammaticality in sentences.

From this, it was logical to assume that because grammatical competence was universal, it must be innate. That is, for each and every one of us to achieve grammatical competence, this linguistic ability must be part of our genetic make-up. To this end, Chomsky (1965) (see also McNeill, 1966) proposed an innate "black box", a Language Acquisition Device or LAD, capable of receiving linguistic input (the sentences of the language in which the child was growing up) and, from these, deriving universal grammatical rules. The child with his innate knowledge of linguistic universals worked from the language spoken (the manifestation of the language referred to as "the surface structure") and derived from this input a grammatical rule system of the particular language to which he is exposed. When articulated, this rule system could account for the production of the rules of the language as well as an awareness of the structure of the language learned.

Chomsky, like Piaget (as will be described later), has an organismic perspective of development—that is, knowledge (or cognition, or language) is universal. Language (or any other cognitive ability such as memory) emerges as a universal property across individuals. While the context is deemed necessary for the knowledge to appear, how it affects the course or sequence of development remains a mystery. Furthermore, interindividual variation, particularly in developmental contexts, is not acknowledged. Universality is a characteristic of Chomsky's theory, broadly shared with Piaget and other organismic theorists.

Bruner's Theory

Bruner's theory of language is aligned with contextual theories of cognitive development such as Bronfenbrenner's (1979) and Vygotsky's (1962, 1978) in so far as it is holistic. For Bruner, both the cognitions and the contexts are judged to be crucial for development. Greater account is taken of the contexts necessary for development to occur and, in some senses, cognitive (and language) development is context-specific. The context can be specified at various levels (see Bronfenbrenner, 1979), but Bruner concerned himself with the child's induction into the culture more broadly defined. The culture itself is constituted via the mastery of language. Language is culturally conventionalised. The optimum entry to the culture is via social interaction with another member of the culture. In the child's case, this is usually the mother, who interacts, talks and communicates with her child. In such a way, the child becomes imbued with the conventions of language—its form and its meaning—in contexts that are familiar and recognisable.

Bruner (1983) proposed that a child learns to use language, rather than learning language *per se*. That is, he emphasised the communicative aspect of language development rather than the structural nature of language. He was concerned with demonstrating the child's capacity to communicate (and not necessarily only through spoken language) with other members of the same culture. Part of learning to communicate involves learning what words and phrases mean. In order to learn the conventional meaning(s) attached to words, the child must engage in interaction with a conversant word user. A further part of learning to communicate involves learning when and where to use these conventionalised meanings, in which social situations certain words are considered appropriate or inappropriate. Children have to learn to recognise contexts of word use. Again, interaction with a variety of people can facilitate this process, as nuances of communication guide the child's attempts to select grammatically correct and socially appropriate words and phrases.

According to Bruner, the child requires two forces to learn to use language. One of these is equivalent to the innate Language Acquisition Device and is an internal "push" force which drives the child to learn language at all. The other force is a "pull" force and is the presence of a supportive environment to assist the learning of language. This support takes the form of another person or persons with whom the child interacts, plus recognisable and regular contexts in which language is used. This framework Bruner called the Language Acquisition Support System (or LASS) and it is essential for the child's learning of language. Adult assistance is a necessary ingredient in the language learning process, and such scaffolding facilitates the child's task. There is a close relationship between the innate capacity of the child to learn language and the social support offered and given to expedite the expression of that endowment. Bruner (1983) aimed to explain how these two forces, in tandem, could be linked both theoretically and empirically to present a comprehensive picture of language development. Studies, including those of Bruner's, which have examined the facilitatory effects of social interaction on language acquisition, especially language viewed as a system of words with meaning and pragmatics, will be described in Chapter 3.

Piaget's Theory

Piaget's theory of cognitive development is well known and well documented (see, for example, Flavell, 1985). What is not so well known is how this theory has been incorporated into a framework that emphasises the social nature of cognitive and linguistic development.

Piaget's theory, like Chomsky's, is organismic. That is, the universality of cognition across domains is stressed and the context is believed relatively unimportant and uninfluential for qualitative changes in cognition. None the less, children are regarded as actively constructing their knowledge. Changes in knowledge or cognition are unidirectional and emerge as the biological nature of the human organism unfolds. To document these changes, Piaget made a myriad of formal and informal observations of the cognitions of infants and children that occurred as they aged and developed. Changes in cognition were regarded as inevitable, unrelenting and irretrievable. Consistencies in performance on an enormous range of cognitive problems tapped by Piaget revealed for him qualitative changes during children's development. These he presented as an integrated theory of cognitive development, which was universal in its applicability and characterised the underlying structure of thinking. His approach was both constructivist and interactionist.

Piaget's theory of development is based on the assumptions that underlie biological growth. Two functional invariants, derived from the natural sciences, account for how information from the environment is dealt with. These mechanisms are *organisation* (i.e. the systematicity and grouping of behaviours and human activities) and *adaptation*. Both are inferred from behaviour and both produce cognitive structures to deal with increasingly complex environments. Adaptation involves assimilation and accommodation, the former being the incorporation of new information into existing structures, whereas the latter refers to the changes in existing structures after contact with novel information. Equilibration refers to the self-regulatory mechanism that co-ordinates assimilation and accommodation. Cognitive structures are the inter-related organisational properties that are actively constructed by the child. They are not based on actual brain or neural structures, but have a rather restricted use in Piaget's theory. Developmentally, the child is construed as going through four stages of structural development, the sensory-motor, the pre-operational, the concrete operational and finally the formal operational. Piaget was concerned with the development of mental operations which were regarded as internal mechanisms and reversible, derived from the child's active engagement with the environment. Development thus proceeded through these stages, marked by qualitative changes in cognitive ability.

Piaget's original theoretical formulations are neither as general nor as robust as he would have led us to believe. The age-related systematic changes in cognitive performance may or may not reflect structural changes in the way children think. This issue is difficult to prove or disprove except that Piaget's position is but one way of characterising cognitive changes, and there are more recent alternatives (see, for example, Karmiloff-Smith, 1986a; and for a summary see Wood, 1988).

Although Piaget considered his theory interactionist, he did not emphasise to any great extent the role of the child's interaction with the environment in the construction of knowledge. This relative neglect of the social environment in particular has been countered recently by studies that demonstrate how social interaction facilitates performance on a range of Piaget's cognitive tasks. These will be considered in depth later in the book. These studies are different to those conducted in the 1970s which sought to "teach" children aspects of cognition (teaching being itself a social event). What transpired from many of the earlier studies was that (a) components of cognitive tasks could be taught but were rarely generalised or long-lasting, and (b) other aspects of cognition, such as language ability and memory, affected children's performance on Piaget's tasks (e.g. Donaldson & Balfour, 1968; Bryant & Trabasso, 1971; Grieve & Garton, 1981). Subsequent research has continued to examine the development of aspects of cognition originally explained by Piaget but by using a more open theoretical and empirical approach (see, for example, reviews by Donaldson, 1978, and Wood, 1988, and the volume edited by Grieve and Hughes, 1991).

Vygotsky's Theory

Vygotsky (1962, 1978, 1986) is a proponent of the contextual approach to development. Holders of contextual orientations to development, including Bruner as discussed earlier, have typically a broader view of development and do not dwell on specifics of language or cognition. They identify with holistic explanations of development whereby the individual and the environment are closely linked. Language and cognition are not discrete units but rather part of a broad spectrum of abilities that emerges during development.

Vygotsky represents a dialectical theorist who emphasises both the cultural aspects of development as well the historical influences. For Vygotsky, reciprocity between the individual and society, the latter being defined both culturally and historically, is important. There is an attempt to specify the causes of developmental change, both in the individual (child) and in society. The context of change and development is the main focus because it is here that we can look for social influences that instigate cognitive and linguistic growth and learning in children.

Vygotsky's theory, although not appearing in English until 1962, was formulated in post-Revolution Russia. The prevailing political and philosophical currents undoubtedly influenced Vygotsky and his thinking, and interested readers are urged to read further (see, for example, Luria, 1976; Wertsch, 1985a, 1985b). The basic tenets to Vygotsky's theory were that speech is social in origin and that language precedes rational thought and influences the nature of thinking. Vygotsky proposed that higher mental functions (namely language and thinking) developed first in the child in interaction with another person. These interpersonal functions gradually became intrapersonal as children realised their significance (both cultural and historical). This theoretical position was congruent with a Marxist perspective on change and development in so far as it gives prominence to social forces that impact on development. The development of language (or speech) permits the child entry into the culture because she can use the conventionalised communication system, passed on via social interaction, and internalised.

One major component of Vygotsky's theory is the fact that "teaching" and "learning" are viewed as two parallel processes in the development of higher mental processes. Indeed the word "obuchenie" in Russian has both meanings (Wertsch, 1984). The instructional component is thus regarded as an integral part of the learning process. In order to learn, there must be teaching geared to the child's existing cognitive level. A supportive "teacher" will find that level and attempt, via the interactive context, to extend the child's ability, knowledge or skill. Appropriate support will be context- and content-dependent but will permit the child to receive responsibility for the regulation, monitoring and maintenance of her behaviour. Generalisability, while not a major issue in Vygotsky's theory, is inevitable once the child has realised the strategic importance of the task-specific behaviours and utilises them subsequently in new contexts.

ENDOGENOUS CONSTRAINTS TO DEVELOPMENT

By assuming that bases of knowledge are both biological and social and that a dynamic interaction between the two results in growth and development, I have up to now ignored the fact that growth can also arise endogenously. According to Karmiloff-Smith (1986a), the growth of knowledge in a range of spheres is an endogenous process whereby there is exploitation of existing information and knowledge. Cognitive development is, in her view, data-driven and results from the use and re-use of already available knowledge in different manifestations. The research question that then arises concerns the constraints on the internal data base that cause it to take such a long developmental time to unfurl. Knowledge is stored as internal modules which operate on the environment in new ways as they themselves change and develop. This view is currently undergoing theoretical refinement and experimental substantiation but represents a different way of considering cognitive and linguistic development (see also Gelman & Baillargeon, 1983; Carey, 1985; Gelman & Markman, 1986; Markman, 1989).

However, this view neglects the active role that the social environment can play in presenting the developing child with conditions appropriate for such internal reorganisation to occur. Learning is regarded solely as the elaboration and modification of existing cognitive procedures for dealing with information from the environment. In all conceptual domains, there is an underlying intuitive or implicit understanding of how to deal with the world, and these understandings are continually reorganised during the early years. However, the instructional aspect is ignored, and it is this very aspect that I wish to place as pivotal to the child's cognitive and linguistic development. Not only formal instruction, but the learning that takes place as a result of interacting with another, perhaps more cognitively competent, member of the same prevailing social and cultural group. Thus, I wish to put aside, for the meantime, the position that deals with the development of endogenous procedural skills and how these may be constraining factors in development and consider instead predominantly social facilitatory factors.

WHAT IS SOCIAL INTERACTION?

It is assumed that social interaction is the fundamental vehicle for the dynamic transmission of cultural and historical knowledge. This book seeks to augment this position by providing a wealth of confirmatory theoretical and empirical data to corroborate this. It is therefore crucial to have a precise definition of social interaction. This book is about social interaction and everybody has notions about what should be involved. None the less, a clear definition of social interaction is imperative so that specific assumptions can be substantiated or challenged. A definition of social interaction states that at a minimum two persons exchanging information are essential. Social interaction further implies some degree of reciprocity and bidirectionality between these participants (although it must be acknowledged that there are degrees of both). Social interaction thus assumes the active involvement of both participants in the interchange, bringing to it different experiences and knowledge, both qualitative and quantitative.

Children generally do not grow up in isolation. There are ample opportunities for children to interact with other people—parents, brothers, sisters, grandparents, aunts and uncles, family friends, other children, other adults—the list is endless. Depending on the culture and other prevailing social conventions, children have varying degrees of social contact with people, each of whom will have some impact on them. Further, other socialisation agents such as television will form part of the developing child's life and, although the degree of the child's active involvement is necessarily less, some influence is inevitable (see, for example, Greenfield, 1984). Children may also have opportunities to interact with unseen persons—they may talk on the telephone or to imaginary companions, or leave notes for Father Christmas—or with "pretend" participants such as teddy bears, dolls and pets whose verbal skills are somewhat lacking. Thus, there are numerous occasions when children engage in active social interactions and it is argued that it is precisely these opportunities that are fundamental to the development of linguistic and cognitive skills and knowledge.

The nature of the child's involvement must be active rather than passive as social interaction as construed in this volume implies degrees of reciprocity and bidirectionality. The relative contribution of the child, and arguably of the "other person", will affect the nature and the outcome of the interaction. This contribution depends on both the existing levels of experience and knowledge as well the nature and purpose of the interaction. In the child's case, her age and existing language and cognitive knowledge will influence the nature and extent of her contribution. It must also be borne in mind that the context and the function of the social interaction will determine the role(s) adopted by the participants and their relative contributions (both expected and actual).

For example, there are differences in an interaction between a mother and her six-day-old baby, between two children playing "spacemen" and between an older sister teaching her younger brother how to count. The content of the interactions is obviously different. The first is purely social and sociable and would probably consist of the mother saying things like "who's a good baby then?" and the infant not showing any outward sign of responding except perhaps to turn her head towards the source of the voice. The second involves the establishment and maintenance of roles between two children of (more or less, depending on the requirements of the game) equal standing in order for the game to proceed. Finally, the last scenario is didactic: The older child is *teaching* the younger child a mathematical concept. None the less, it can be argued that each of these social interactions is facilitating the growth of new knowledge in at least one of the participants. In the first interaction described, the infant is beginning to recognise her mother and mother's voice; in the second interaction, one—if not both—of the children is learning about what spacemen do (or at least are expected to do in the context of the game being played); and in the third interaction, the objective is solely the advancement of the knowledge of the younger participant. On the basis of such observations, as well as through experimentation, it has been claimed that social interaction indeed facilitates cognitive and linguistic development (for example, see Bearison, 1982; Light, 1983; Murray, 1983; and chapters in Bornstein & Bruner, 1989). Any stronger causal role for social interaction in the development of knowledge has proved difficult to sustain, largely because the mechanisms are hard to identify, quantify and qualify with any degree of precision.

In this book, the type of social interaction on which I shall be focusing predominantly is *dyadic interaction*. The pair, or dyad, is the smallest microcosm of social interaction. The dyad is also the easiest group to study experimentally since the direct influence of each participant on the other can be measured carefully and accurately. Most of the studies that are reported in this book have the dyad as their focus. In the studies of language, the dyads tend to be composed of a mother and her child. That is not to say there are no studies that have examined the influence that other caregivers, family members or friends might have on a child's language development. Rather it is a reflection of the fact that the mother is still the predominant caregiver and is hence usually the most available and amenable to experimental study. In most studies the mother is indeed the major participant, but it is important to bear in mind that the terms "significant" and "more competent other" can usually be substituted, at least at a general and theoretical level. Where appropriate throughout this book, the term "adult" is used to convey this generalised notion.

Methodologically, studies of social influences on language development have tended to be observational and naturalistic (or quasi-naturalistic), with the dyads being observed in as "normal" a situation as possible. Observations are often conducted in the child's home or in the laboratory, equipped with home paraphernalia such as toys and books, chairs and cushions. The interactions are usually videotaped, sometimes additionally audiotaped and/or supplemented with note-taking or the checking of predetermined coding sheets. The more naturalistic method is most suitable both for language research as well as for research requiring the younger children who typically participate in language production studies. Studies of language development in older children, however, are usually experimental and examine language comprehension rather than production (Garton & Pratt, 1989).

In contrast, most of the studies of social influences on children's cognitive development have used dyads composed of two children. Very often these children are matched on the basis of similar or different ages, similar or different cognitive levels (as measured by a pre-test for example) or similar or different sexes. The children then work together on a task where the solution is known to only one member of the dyad or to neither of them. Measures of cognitive development are generally based on the manner in which children come to solve the problem and the robustness of their solution(s). In most cases the outcome, after social interaction, is a cognitive gain for the less competent child. The precise focus of the research depends on the theoretical orientation adopted—Piagetian inspired research focusing on the measurable cognitive gains (the outcome) and Vygotskian inspired research focusing on the processes of the interaction and the transfer, or sharing, of responsibility during the task solution.

In such studies of cognitive development, the approach is best characterised as experimental, with tight investigative control over the materials available to the children. Careful experimental design and variable manipulation ensure that maximally useful data are collected. In contrast to the observational methods, the older children who most often participate in research on cognitive development are more amenable to such stricter experimental control.

However, this dichotomy between naturalistic language development research and the experimental study of cognitive development neglects the large body of work that has examined the development of cognition through social interaction. Many of the roots of cognitive development can be traced back to early social interactions between mothers and their children. Much of early development through social interaction involves both language and cognition. For example, work by Durkin and colleagues (e.g. Durkin, Shire, Riem, Crowther & Rutter, 1986) examines early number use in an interactive, communicative context. Such research crosses the traditional boundaries between language and cognition through an examination of the social and linguistic contexts of early cognitive competencies.

In conclusion, the four theories described in this chapter have all been major influences on the study of the relationship between social interaction and cognitive and linguistic development. The impact may have been indirect as in Chomsky's theory, influential as source material as in Piaget's theory and probably Vygotsky's theory in so far as neither conducted experiments specifically to test their theoretical formulations in this domain, or direct as in Bruner's theory which has been applied and tested explicitly. None the less, each has been an important driving force behind a body of research each of which may seem disparate from the other but which I shall attempt to reconcile in a theoretical overview.

The next four chapters will extend the original formulations of these theorists through illustrative research studies and by drawing attention to theoretical shifts and their interpretations in contemporary developmental studies. In Chapters 2 and 3, the predominant focus is on language development. In Chapter 2, I describe research studies that have concentrated on the relationship between language input and language development. Language input is described in terms of the person providing such input to the child rather than dealing rather narrowly with the language *per se*. In the main, the focus is on the mother as the supplier of language input. In Chapter 3, the attention shifts to an examination of broader forms of social assistance to the child language learner. These encompass not only social structures but also ways in which the child is predisposed from birth to interact socially with others. Such innate abilities are both required for and encourage social interaction, thus preparing a way into the social world. In addition, such propensities provide a basis for the infant to learn from the resultant social interaction.

Chapters 4 and 5 examine cognitive development. In Chapter 4, the theoretical positions formulated by Piaget and Vygotsky respectively are described. Experimental studies on cognitive conflict and cognitive growth influenced by Piaget's theory are presented, illustrating the scope of the theory and the range of the research. In addition, research examining cognitive tasks as social interaction is described. Likewise, studies directly influenced by Vygotsky's theory are described, focusing on the scope of the theory and the diverse nature of the concomitant theoretical and empirical work. Recent research, reviewed in Chapter 5, has attempted to compare and contrast both positions and to reconcile them into a broader theoretical perspective. Communicative and collaborative social interaction is regarded as the catalyst for improved cognitive performance and the final chapters of this book provide strong evidence for such a position.

A final summing-up chapter concludes the book, drawing together the major themes that emerge. A theoretical framework, arguing for the inclusion of social mediating mechanisms in language and cognitive development, is sketched, together with some recent research extensions in the applied domain.

CHAPTER TWO

Language Input and Language Development

This chapter is concerned with the nature of language spoken to young children and the influence this has on how language is acquired by children, the structure of children's language and the functions of language. The starting point is Chomsky's theory of language, described briefly in Chapter 1.

A DEFINITION OF LANGUAGE

For the purposes of this chapter I have initially adopted a narrow definition of language, namely the structure of language, in line with Chomsky's formal theory of language, and I shall consider how linguistic input affects and influences a child's subsequent grammatical development. The assumption underlying this position is that language as a structural system is independent of language as a communicative system. The focus to begin with is on how the structure of language (its form by and large, but also its meaning) is learned and how this process might be facilitated by the nature of the language spoken to the child. Although studies of social interaction and language development have tended to view language as communication, early research in the field was dominated by Chomsky's structural theory. A marked shift in emphasis occurred once the social aspects of the acquisition process became obvious. While there may be examples of explicit teaching of grammar (by mothers, or by teachers), in this book the relationship between input and development is regarded as being less formal, possibly less explicit but perhaps more powerful. As well as the structure of language being learned (as evidenced through the production of grammatical speech), language forms can be related to meaning. This relationship, its direction and its nature, will be considered later in this chapter. Thus the focus shifts from the form of the language learned by the developing child to the meaning, content, and uses of that language and hence to language as communication.

In recent times, Chomsky's theory has served as an important catalyst for research in language development in two divergent ways. His relative neglect of the social environment in which language was developing led to a huge upsurge of research in the 1970s examining the properties of the input language that might facilitate or impede language development. Much of this research and its spin-offs will be considered in depth in this chapter. It is interesting initially to note however that there are different strands to such research, some considering broader aspects such as the nature of input language and how it correlates with children's language development and more recent research examining specific speech adjustments by adults and their particular impact on defined emergent structures in the child's language.

The second contemporary influence of Chomsky's theory is seen in work on parameter setting in linguistics. Parameter setting acknowledges the innate aspect of language acquisition in so far as the child is genetically endowed with grammatical rules or principles. What is important is that at least some, if not all, of the rules are under-specified, or given at such a level of generality that they require specification. In Chomsky's original theory, children were innately predisposed to write the rules of the grammar, by selecting their rules from an infinite number that might exist. In a parameter setting model, children instead set the value of a parameter in a universal grammatical rule. Most of the impetus for this turnaround derived from the rather obvious observation that both the input data to LAD and the output from LAD consist only of positive exemplars of grammatical rules. The "no-negative evidence" hypothesis means that children rarely encounter utterances that would violate the rules entertained. Children are neither misunderstood nor corrected when they produce ungrammatical language nor do parents produce (by and large) ungrammatical sentences.

In specifying a parameter, or fixing a grammatical rule, a child learns from the abundance of positive and uncorrected evidence for that rule and sets the parameter accordingly. So far, most of the research has been at the interface of pure linguistics and language acquisition. Studies such as those by Hyams (1986) have attempted to describe the initial setting for parameters, settings that can be altered later in the face of "triggering" data. The initial settings may be universal, and as such are confirmed or disconfirmed by the language, causing restructuring of the current grammar.

A correlate of parameter setting is learnability (Atkinson, 1987; Gleitman & Wanner, 1988), which is "how linguistic representations are attained given the limited data base available" (Borer & Wexler, 1987, p. 123). This is a broader conceptualisation of language learning than parameter setting. Learnability theory makes two broad assumptions—one, that formal grammatical principles are innate, and two, that the language can be learned and adult language is the ideal to be attained. Learnability theory attempts to account for how language is constructed under such circumstances. According to learnability theory, the child is equipped with an innate set of grammatical principles, a range of places where variation can occur (i.e. parameters that can be set) and a learning procedure. With these, there must also be no negative evidence, no explicit teaching of the grammar, the data to enable learning are simple, and the options open to the child learner are very restricted. It is believed (e.g. Gleitman & Wanner, 1988; Menyuk, 1988) that learnability can account for the acquisition of language in a plausible way and in a manner consistent with other cognitive developments.

A further fundamental assumption concerning the nature of language, which must be made at least to set the research in perspective, is that language is a biological endowment which requires some environmental stimulation for instigation. This assumption is not unrelated to the previous point. In this context, what is usually meant by language is linguistic rules, universal rules that determine grammaticality of speech. These linguistic rules are powerful, abstract, generalisable formulations permitting the specification of acceptable (i.e. grammatically correct) sentences of the language. The rules are implicit, but may become explicit on request, if an error has been made or when a judgement of grammaticality is required. Evidence for the development of these rules is usually established via the child's spoken language, where consistent and explicable errors as well as the production of grammatical utterances indicate the grasp of a certain linguistic rule. An account of how language develops from a biological perspective thus focuses on the acquisition of specific linguistic rules and their manifestation in the spoken language.

Language Development

According to Chomsky (1965) and McNeill (1966, 1970), language development comprised the output of LAD, the mysterious "black box" component of language acquisition. This output was the linguistic rules of the current language community. In terms of explaining *how* language develops, a biological, innate perspective focuses on the creation by the child of abstract linguistic rules. This is at the expense of the other factors in the LAD equation, namely, the input and the child herself. Scant respect was paid to the linguistic input which Chomsky (1965) regarded as deficient and degenerate. Thus, for all its shortcomings, the language input to the child paid little or no part in the acquisition process. Its role was limited to either triggering the innate LAD or of influencing the subsequent direction (and speed) of the process (see Wells & Robinson, 1982).

However, it soon became obvious, particularly to those concerned with children's development rather than linguistic development solely, that this focus while not necessarily "wrong" was myopic. Additional assumptions must be made to illustrate that input language does indeed play a major part in how children acquire language. To this end, it must be demonstrated that aspects of the input speech are causally related to the child's speech, as evidenced by either the presence or the absence of specific features. Thus, it is important also to examine the input variables, specifically the contribution of the *linguistic* input variables, in a language acquisition model. It is, in addition, equally important to include child variables in an acquisition model purporting to describe how language develops. A child's cognitive level or abilities may also play a vital role, either facilitatory or constraining, in how language develops.

Chomsky's theory of language, and the subsequent model of acquisition, further assumed that language developed automatically and instantaneously. In its strongest form, this hypothesis is false given that children do not suddenly learn to use language (and grammatically correct language at that). The acquisition process takes a number of years, involves the making of mistakes, and indeed it may take longer to acquire language, defined as adult language, than previously thought—see Durkin (1986), Karmiloff-Smith (1986b), and Garton and Pratt (1989) for discussions of some of the issues relating to later language development. With the admission that language development is a gradual process came the acknowledgement that there were other important considerations that were relevant. If we maintain a view of language as involving three components—input, output and the child's capacity in between—then questions arise in each domain. These questions concern changes that occur over time that might influence or affect how language is learned or how language develops.

The actual input language spoken to the child may well change as the child moves from the prelinguistic stage, through identifiable phases of language development, until adult levels of competence are reached. Such changes in linguistic knowledge, usually perceived as increments, will themselves influence the nature of the input language. In addition, the child's cognitive capacity increases, for example through improved memory capabilities and through improved and more efficient uses of language, which will impact on subsequent language learning. The three components of language development are inter-related so intimately that it is difficult to think they were originally studied in isolation. Developmental psycholinguists have endeavoured to answer the question of how the input variables change over time, by examining both the actual linguistic structures directed to children as they develop, and also by examining variables relating to the person, most often the mother, who talks to the child. Together, the study of these variables has been termed variously "baby talk", "motherese" and "child directed speech" (CDS) (Snow, 1986).

LANGUAGE SPOKEN TO CHILDREN

The terms "baby talk", "motherese" and "child directed speech" have been used by and large interchangeably and sometimes imprecisely. Fundamental to all concepts is the notion of an adult, or significant, more competent other, who more often than not is the mother. Thus the primary research target has been on maternal speech, without, theoretically at least, ignoring the contribution other family members and friends make to a child's language development. I have used the terms in a non-overlapping manner to reflect a progressive research concern with both dyadic participants, moving from research attention being directed towards the form of the input language produced by the mother, through to a closer examination of the form and functions of maternal speech, to a broader perspective incorporating aspects of the social interaction between mother and child. To these three, I intend adding a new fourth category, namely "child interactive speech", which I will explain after a description of the more traditional ways of categorising language spoken to children.

Baby Talk

In differentially labelling the characteristic speech addressed to young children, it is understood that this language represents a modification of that used under normal circumstances. Language addressed to children typically consists of short, but grammatical, sentences, lots of repetitions, a slow rate of delivery, syntactic simplicity, higher pitch and exaggerated intonation, and a greater number of questions and imperatives than would usually be the case (see, for example, Snow, 1972; Sachs, Brown & Salerno, 1976; Cross, 1977; Wells & Robinson,

1982). In addition, baby talk is further characterised by the inclusion of infantile lexical items such as "pussy" or "choo-choo". Such apparent simplifications are often used because the original word is judged to be too hard to pronounce, e.g. "tummy" for stomach, because the syllable reduplication occurs spontaneously in the child's speech ("dada" then used to refer to father) or because there is a recognisable commonly used word such as "pussy". Simplified speech may even incorporate neologisms, originally coined by the child but adopted by the parent(s) when speaking to the child. Such simplified lexical items are unique to baby talk and are not included in subsequent characterisations of the language addressed to children (Garton & Pratt, 1989).

The notion that baby talk is in any way badly formed syntactically or semantically has been well disproved. As noted, language addressed to children is simplified, well formed and by and large meaningful. It is also relevant to young children as it tends to focus on the "here and now" both temporally and spatially. It is also highly redundant, with its large number of repetitions, rephrasings and paraphrasings (Snow, 1972). Language addressed to children is clearly different from speech addressed to other adults, but seems to be adjusted to match young children's language levels.

What does determine the adjustments or modifications of speech that are made? Are the simplifications and redundancies systematic? How do the modifications affect the child's own linguistic development? It seems that, broadly, if we consider baby talk (and the research literature available to inform us on this particular way of characterising speech addressed to children), speech adjustments are made on the basis of the age of the child (Cross, 1977; Snow, 1977). The age of the child reflects the stage of her development which an adult can identify and which leads to conceptions about the child's level of understanding and linguistic ability. The use of baby talk is not specific to a particular child but rather is tied to general expectations about a child's developmental level, based not only on linguistic abilities but also on cognitive, social and physical attributes.

It can also be stated that speech adjustments are made in response to the reactions of the child listener to the language spoken. Children do apparently attend and respond to language that is simpler both grammatically and in terms of the vocabulary used. Shipley, Gleitman and Smith (1969) found that children did not attend to adults' language that was more complicated than their own or unfamiliar to them. It was further believed that this selective attention to simple language explained why children neither responded to nor became misled by conversations involving only adults or by TV and radio broadcasts. Such language was too difficult and the child dealt with this by tuning out.

Thus, modifications are made in order to communicate and converse with young children, using language to which they can attend and respond. Snow (1986) takes this argument one step further with the implication that language addressed to children must therefore be well attuned and adapted to the child's linguistic level. The characteristics of this fine-tuned simplified speech would thus change dramatically when the child's comprehension of language becomes obvious (sometime towards the end of the first year of life) and then alter progressively as the child ages and her linguistic level increases. Knowledge of the child's production and/or comprehension system is required to permit an estimate of the optimal level of fine-tuning necessary at any point in time to facilitate language development.

The nomenclature has changed since the adoption of the term "baby talk" by language researchers in the early 1970s, but essentially the concept that systematic modifications of speech take place when young children are addressed by others remains the same. The emphasis has shifted from an examination and description of adjusted speech, to variables associated with the mother's contribution, with more recent research focusing on the child as an active processor of this linguistic input directed to her. It is believed that speech adjustments occur as a result of a speaker communicating directly to young children (Snow, 1972), although there is additional evidence that simplifications of speech occur when a speaker is addressing any linguistically naive person (Romaine, 1984), including foreigners (Warren-Leubecker & Bohannon, 1982), the intellectually handicapped (Pratt, Bumstead & Raines, 1976) and pets (Hirsh-Pasek & Treiman, 1983). Further, it has been found (e.g. Shatz & Gelman, 1973) that language adjustments are not only made by mothers and fathers, but by anyone addressing young children, including four- and five-year-old speakers. This finding suggested the assumption that baby talk is universal and indeed it has been described in cultures other than middle-class English-speaking ones (see, for example, Wells & Robinson, 1982).

The earliest baby talk research was aimed at cataloguing those aspects of language that characterise speech addressed to young children. In addition, this research opened up the debate over the relative influence of the innate component of language and the environmental component in determining language development. Certainly, the research did not refute Chomsky's model of acquisition, but it convincingly altered the emphasis by pointing out that the input language while being structurally less complex than that usually spoken must have an impact on how language develops. However, what was not yet established was the precise impact these simplifications had nor the relative influence of the innate and the environmental (or social) components. The earliest studies were purely descriptive and paid little heed either to the content of the language spoken or the uses to which the language was being put, save in a broad structural sense (e.g. the incidence of question forms and imperatives). The study of baby talk focused on the input language without consideration being given to the person producing the language nor the child who received the language. Research then shifted to a closer examination of the relationship between the input language as produced by the mother and the child's processing and use of that linguistic information. This change of direction was marked by the adoption of the term "motherese" to refer to language addressed to children.

Motherese

"Motherese" describes the speech of mothers to their children. The original impetus for the shift in emphasis for the language input studies was the notion that perhaps adults in general, and mothers in particular, were somehow supplying their children with "language lessons". The problem with this position is that it represents an unsubstantiated generalisation from the research studies. None the less, the suggestion that mothers were perhaps unwittingly performing a teaching function in modifying their language in relation to some aspect of their child's development (possibly their age as speculated previously) spawned a decade of research examining the characteristics of maternal speech that might be related to progress in language development. Snow (1986) dismisses this interpretation as an oversimplification and claims speech modifications by mothers are merely the result of mothers trying to communicate with their small offspring rather than explicitly teaching them to talk.

Some maternal speech is well documented as being an attempt to teach talk (Cazden, 1983). For example, parents are concerned with the teaching of pragmatic rules such as social greetings ("hello") and conventions ("thank you") and will go to great lengths to ensure young children produce these utterances at socially appropriate times. These items tend to be taught explicitly. Mothers also have been noted to teach their children labels for objects (Brown, 1958; Ninio & Bruner, 1978), although as Wells and Robinson (1982) point out, labelling is never the most important function of adult speech to children. However, parents also occasionally correct the language used by their children, both the grammar and actual word chosen, although they are typically more concerned with the content veracity of their children's language than with the structure or the adherence to linguistic rules (Brown & Hanlon, 1970; Pinker, 1986).

The question still remains of what role maternal speech, or adjusted speech in general, plays in the development of a child's language. This issue can be examined at a number of different levels, each of which has stimulated research. The topics are inter-related, and indeed some of the data have been reanalysed from a different perspective at a later date. Some researchers have claimed that modified maternal speech is causally related to child language level and that this relationship is evidenced at both the syntactic and the semantic levels. Causal relationships have been quite difficult to establish, and most researchers have contented themselves with finding correlations, if anything. Even so, these correlations have not always been positive. So, for example, Cross (1977) and Newport, Gleitman and Gleitman (1977) failed to find positive correlations between every measure of maternal speech (including measures of structural complexity and intelligibility) and children's developing grammar (coded via measures of syntactic complexity such as mean length of utterance (MLU) and use of auxiliary structures). It was subsequently claimed mothers did not fine-tune their language syntactically to their child's developing productive abilities since there was no evidence to support this position (Cross, 1979; Gleitman, Newport & Gleitman, 1984). Cross did however find a relationship between maternal speech and children's comprehension of language. In addition, some studies have found no relationship between maternal speech input and children's semantic development (e.g. Snow, 1977). More fine-grained subsequent analyses have begun to tease out what may be specific correlations during development, especially when maternal language addressed to children is regarded merely as a sub-set of all adult language (see Ninio & Snow, 1988, for a resumé). That is, it is claimed that children are exposed to a restricted range of vocabulary items, sentence types and grammatical constructions. Each discrete subsystem of rules has its linguistic realisation in one communicative function (Ninio & Snow, 1988). Such simplicity in the correspondence between linguistic form and function must then relate to the communicative system created and used by the child.

The Motherese Hypothesis

The motherese hypothesis was constructed to provide a testable hypothesis about the impact maternal speech has on a child's developing language structures. Its clearest articulation occurs in the 1984 paper of Gleitman, Newport and Gleitman (p. 45), where the motherese hypothesis is defined as "the hypothesis that the(se) SPECIAL properties of caretaker speech play a causal role in acquisition". In proposing this hypothesis, researchers were attempting to answer the question of whether a mother's speech affects a child's developing language, and if so, how. This is a different perspective on the language learning puzzle to that discussed earlier which focused more on the extent to which a mother's linguistic input is adjusted (fine-tuned) to the child's developing linguistic (syntactic and semantic) capabilities. The focus has shifted to the impact the linguistic input has on the development of the structure and complexity of language.

Rather than seeing motherese as speech different from or as a simplification of ordinary speech, Gleitman et al. (1984) believe it restricts the range of forms and functions available for children to choose from. Maternal language use does not vary dramatically during the first three years of a child's life. None the less, the motherese hypothesis has not gone unchallenged (e.g. Newport et al., 1977; Gleitman et al., 1984; Furrow & Nelson, 1986, who argue for consideration to be given to biases in the child learner rather than the mother's language) or unmitigated. It is claimed that the general effect is stable, and maternal speech, by its very restrictive nature, influences language development by the child's differential exploitation of particular linguistic structures at different times. Likewise, it challenges a fine-tuning hypothesis, claiming stability of input. It should be noted finally that a weaker, non-contentious, version of the hypothesis states that maternal speech facilitates rapid language learning.

Thus, an issue that has dominated the literature on the motherese hypothesis concerns the extent to which the hypothesis reflects whether mothers fine-tune their language to the child's developing language (Cross, 1977) or whether indeed the reverse occurs, namely that mothers do not change their language as the child develops, but that learning is the result of the child exploiting some of the language some of the time (Gleitman et al., 1984). The hypotheses entertained are a consequence of achieving positive and negative correlations between elements in a mother's language and elements that subsequently appear in a child's language. Maternal linguistic complexity, rate and lexical diversity have been shown to be positively related to features of children's developing language. For example, syntactic measures such as the mother's use of Wh- questions, Yes/No questions and tag questions were found to be correlated with MLU (sentence length) measures (Cross, 1979). In addition, mothers' use of nouns and pronouns (the proportions of pronouns and noun-phrases per utterance) was found to be correlated with children's expressive vocabulary (as measured by the type-token ratio of lexical diversity). Other studies have provided evidence of the broad success of imitations plus expansions for producing language gains (Newport et al., 1977; Cross, 1979).

While these correlational studies have tended to show that the relative prevalence of certain features in maternal speech is associated with children's language growth, they have not demonstrated the effects of specific language inputs. Experimental studies that systematically include or exclude particular language features are the only source of direct evidence of the effect of language input. Nelson and his colleagues (e.g. Nelson, Carskaddon & Bonvillian, 1973; Nelson, 1977; Baker & Nelson, 1984) conducted a series of such studies. In this research, children's language is systematically recast by experimenters. Recasts change the syntactic form of the language while maintaining the intended meaning. For example, a child may say "Want a biscuit" which the adult might then recast as "Do you want a biscuit?". However, the length of the utterance remains much the same. Specific language effects can then be examined directly as utterances are selected for recasting and the subsequent impact on the child's own language production monitored. In general, previously unused grammatical forms are noted in the child's language after their use in the experimental recasts.

Other aspects of the child's language such as the length of the utterance produced can be taken into account demonstrating that the effect is specifically grammatical. However because the effects are so specific, it is questionable whether the grammatical development is real or simply reflects parroting of the input (Hoff-Ginsberg & Shatz, 1982). More fundamentally, Bates, Bretherton, Beeghly-Smith and McNew (1983) queried whether the experimental setting and the precise recasting of children's utterances reflected what happened naturally between a mother and her child.

Adults sometimes provide children with negative feedback or criticism of badly constructed language. Actual corrections of grammar (syntax) are rarely recorded in adult–child conversations and greater concern is often expressed over the truthfulness of children's utterances. Clearly, such negative feedback cannot be a consistent source of linguistic knowledge for the child. If requests for clarification (of intent) are counted as negative feedback, then research studies have shown that indeed these may be a more powerful mechanism for corrections and changes to a child's productive language (e.g. Hirsh-Pasek, Treiman & Schneiderman, 1984; Penner, 1987). Adults apparently respond with requests for clarification more often to grammatically ill-formed sentences than to grammatically accurate sentences (with some exceptions). Negative feedback in the form of clarification requests might therefore constitute a source of information regarding the grammatical correctness of language and children might be able to use such information to generate correct sentences. Other sources of feedback include repetitions with expansion and clarification and affirmation with correction (Snow, 1989), both of which have been shown to encourage grammatical corrections in the child's language.

In general, the correlational studies suggest that the modifications mothers (and other adults) make to their language have some impact on children's language development. The majority of the studies supports the position that adults make these modifications in the light of some characteristic(s) of their developing children. Adults certainly simplify their language, expand and recast children's language and also restrict the semantic complexity of their language. They also provide (negative) feedback to ill-formed sentences via clarification requests. On the other hand, from the results of Gleitman et al.'s (1984) study, there is evidence to suggest the opposite: Simplified motherese speech does not change with the child's language level. The child acts as the arbiter of the language selected and used. There is no relationship between the complexity of maternal language and learning. What emerges however is a theory of language learning that presupposes the child is an active participant in the language interactions, selecting and utilising the input they can deal with most successfully. The motherese hypothesis cannot be disconfirmed as it is too general a statement. Correlational evidence is almost always confirmatory. Some more specific theory of language learning needs to supplant the hypothesis, a theory that accounts for the whole process of language learning. According to Gleitman et al. (1984), the active information-processing child is necessary, selectively attending to, using and retaining input language and generating grammatical hypotheses.

From Syntax to Semantics and Pragmatics

It is now widely accepted as a general principle that the focus of language learning ought to be on the dyad. Without wholly neglecting the role of the input and the adult, consideration should instead be given to the child and to the process of learning. All aspects of the language learning "equation" must be included in an account of the acquisition process. In addition, it is apparent that language cannot simply be characterised as linguistic or grammatical rules that require learning. For example, Cross (1977) remarked on the fine-tuning of maternal speech to discourse and pragmatic features in children's language rather than to syntactic complexity. Other studies have focused on the role of semantics or meaning in language acquisition (see Hoff-Ginsberg & Shatz, 1982, for a review). In this case, the situation is more complex since the theoretical underpinnings for semantic development are less clear-cut than for syntactic development. Hence there is little direct research on the topic. The focus has shifted to what is considered the major problem for language development, namely the mapping of form (syntax) with function (semantics) (see Carey, 1982, and Gleitman & Wanner, 1988, for reviews). Studies have examined semantic organisation (e.g. Carey, 1978), semantic categories (Bowerman, 1977) and constraints on word meaning (Markman & Hutchinson, 1984), as well as strategies for learning word meanings such as lexical contrast (Clark, 1987, 1988, 1991), form class (Gelman & Markman, 1986; Taylor & Gelman, 1988), fast mapping (Hiebeck & Markman, 1987), mutual exclusivity bias (Merriman & Bowman, 1989) and quick incidental learning of words (QUIL) (Rice, 1990). There is an obviously different emphasis to the debate surrounding semantic development, with the child's active contribution being paramount and the role of the adult and the input language being less clearly specified.

One major consideration in the study of semantics is the restricted nature of the language spoken to children. The language is very closely tied to the "here and now", and adults when addressing children tend to talk in the present tense, refer to visible objects and comment on on-going activities (Snow et al., 1976). This restricted range of semantic contents may facilitate the beginning stages of language development, as adults try to tie their language specifically to a limited range of circumstances. Such limitations may also serve to explain the restricted syntax used, because present tense utterances tend to be brief statements or questions, whereas comments tend to refer to the colour, the action, or location of the intended referent. Thus there is no need to use complex language when the functions being fulfilled are restricted in scope. Snow (1986) suggests that syntactic simplicity in maternal speech is an artifact of semantic simplicity.

Ninio and Snow (1988, p. 12) use the characteristic of syntactic and semantic simplicity of input speech as a working hypothesis for the study of language acquisition. That is, via noticing what they term "a higher than usual degree of form–function correspondence" in maternal input language, they claim that the input the child is presented with and presumably working on is a limited set of linguistic realisations of specific functions. That is, the formal language used in addressing young children marks precisely some underlying communicative function. This, they argue, implies that the child's early productions are manifestations of this principle whereby communicative intention is mapped directly onto formal linguistic expression. Therefore, communicative intention can validly be used as a way of categorising children's own early utterances. This pragmatic analysis is illustrated by early productive language and Ninio and Snow (1988) believe it has more to offer than a syntactic or semantic theory. Close form-to-function mapping in maternal speech would facilitate not just syntactic development but more particularly semantic development. This proposal is consonant with mechanisms such as lexical contrast, fast mapping and mutual exclusivity bias as children maintain that a difference in form corresponds to a difference in function. The meaning, or set of meanings, for one word does not overlap with those of another word. Merriman and Bowman (1989) discuss a range of theoretical perspectives in relation to mutual exclusivity bias although there is no definitive perspective that can be accorded theory status yet. Research in the area of how children acquire word meaning is currently proving fruitful (Clark, 1991) with the application of pragmatic principles to account for lexical development.

A pragmatic analysis of both input language and the child's subsequent productions permits the taking into account of the seemingly endless variables that can influence the relationship between input and output (as realised in both production and understanding). For example, it may be that the child's *age* is a crucial moderating variable in the study of the relationship between input speech and language development. Studies that have found the highest correlations have involved children who have begun to produce structural utterances (i.e. sentences greater than one word in length). Amongst the highest partial correlations between maternal speech and child language growth (partialling out initial child language level) found by Gleitman et al. (1984) were those between mothers' use of declaratives and the number of verbs used by children per utterance (.98) for younger children (aged between 18 and 21 months). In the case of children aged around 24 months, the highest partial correlations were between mothers' use of Yes/No questions and children's mean length of utterance (MLU) (.92), and mothers' use of Yes/No questions and children's use of verb phrases with auxiliaries (.91).

Gleitman et al.'s (1984) research involved a re-analysis of their data as a rejoinder to Furrow, Nelson and Benedict (1979) whose research had been conducted with younger subjects than the original Newport et al. (1977) study. It may well be that at these lower levels of productive language, structurally simpler input language facilitates the child's grasp of vocabulary and easy syntactic rules (such as pluralisation and progressive verb endings). In pre-syntactic stages perhaps the labelling function is important, providing the child with a functional set of words as building blocks for subsequent, more difficult structural aspects of language. At later stages, when the child has mastered the basics of syntax and semantics and is beginning to acquire more abstract linguistic rules as well as more subtle pragmatic functions, then more complex input may be required. Modified adult speech may be insufficient for the instantiation of formal linguistic rules. These rules may be derived from the earlier models of language constructed by the child which may have been influenced by the nature of the input. It is precisely the formal properties of language that constrain or affect the speed of the child's learning of language, and it may be these formal properties that are the most difficult and complex to adduce.

In addition, the context in which an adult's language is used, and hence interpreted by the child, may influence the rate and course of acquisition. A child must be able to interpret what is being said to them in order both to attend to and respond to, and be likely to learn anything about, language. The pragmatic function of language is, I believe, the most important. Studies of motherese have tended to use particular situations as their focus. Some of these, e.g. a bookreading situation where a mother and her child are totally engrossed in one activity, and one which is highly verbal, may provide a different picture of the nature of maternal input than language used in a different context—for instance, at bathtime. In the former, the child may have an expected role in the interaction and the mother may regard her function as didactic; in the latter, the prime aim of the interaction may be to cleanse the child—a ritual in itself—and the language used by the mother may be for admonition and encouragement (even praise). Furthermore, mothers themselves have different language styles (Nelson, 1973; Goldfield & Snow, 1985) and some mothers are simply more talkative than others. These individual differences, which become manifest in cross-sectional correlational studies of the influence of maternal speech on children's language development, undoubtedly affect the rate, the nature and the course of any child's language development. Although the extent to which children are exposed to a variety of input speech will itself vary, a side product, perhaps a benefit, of these individual differences, is that any child will be exposed to a range of input languages and learn to extrapolate from different speech styles. Such flexibility will have a practical value in later life.

There were, during the 1970s, many studies of motherese and its potentially causal relationship with children's subsequent language development. The primary focus was always on the nature of the maternal, or input, language, rather than on the child as an active listener and creator of language. Despite strong theoretical attempts, such as the use of the motherese hypothesis, to speculate about the role of maternal speech on children's syntactic and semantic development, it has only been those studies which have taken into consideration and accommodated the important individual differences in conversational interaction that have paved the way for more recent studies.

Additional research has been undertaken to demonstrate that paternal as well as maternal speech may impact on children's language development (e.g. Golinkoff & Ames, 1979; Lewis & Gregory, 1987). Also, family constellation and size may affect the nature of language addressed to young children (e.g. Jones & Adamson, 1987; Vandell & Wilson, 1987). An account that can transcend, or incorporate, some or all of these variables, would offer a more useful perspective on the relationship between input language, as measured syntactically, semantically or pragmatically, and children's developing use of appropriate linguistic forms and functions. There is the hint of a change in direction with the more recently adopted phrase "child directed speech", which begins to shift the onus for language development from the adult addressing the child to the child himself as an active conversational participant and creator of language.

Child Directed Speech

This phrase seems to have been widely adopted in recent times, although broadly it encompasses much of what was discussed in relation to baby talk and motherese. It was coined largely to avoid the use of the earlier imprecise neologisms (Snow, 1986). Again it focuses on the adjusted speech input but the child's perspective is taken rather than dwelling on the adult or the nature of the input. Although the phrase "child directed speech" might be interpreted to imply a one-way process from the adult, the shift in focus to the child in the interaction is a promising one. The facilitatory nature of this speech for language development is highlighted, and the social aspects of the necessary conversational interactions are also taken into account. Both the adult and the child are regarded as vital components of the language learning process. The use of the phrase "child directed speech" places the research subsumed under this heading firmly in the social interactionist tradition. The argument is that an adult's language directed to the child facilitates the child's language development because the adult is acting as a conversational partner and is actively involving the child in the verbal interchange (Snow, 1986, 1989).

Snow (1989) compares four features of social interaction that are potentially facilitative for language development. Three of these features, namely fine-tuning, recasts and negative feedback, have already been discussed in this chapter. Of these three, the available research evidence suggests that only recasting actually facilitates language acquisition. Both negative feedback and fine-tuning are potentially facilitative, but require more research to confirm their effectiveness. Evidence for the efficacy of negative feedback is accumulating and Snow (1989, pp. 92-93) is optimistic about the contribution feedback can make to language development: "there is ... every reason to believe that it can and should facilitate language acquisition". The claimed effectiveness of fine-tuning as a facilitator of language development may lie in its contribution towards the establishment of joint attention.

Joint attention is the fourth feature of social interaction that Snow invokes as being important for language acquisition. Joint attention is the mutual establishment of a shared activity, monitored by either the adult or the child in the interaction. Early joint attention has been hypothesised to be related to later language development (Bruner, 1983), as the creation of a joint context permits conversational focus on the same topic. For example, early pointing behaviour by the child directs the mother's attention to a distal object, which she will then name. The language (its form and its function) is heavily dependent on the context created, in this case, by the child. The adult is thus monitoring the child's attentional focus (which alters with age in spatial location and the means used to achieved it) and thence tunes her language accordingly.

Tomasello and Todd (1983) report that the frequency of joint attention between mother–infant pairs is a good predictor of vocabulary growth because the conditions for the learning of words are determined by the child and the context supports such learning. Both the adult and the child can direct the other's attention and this flexibility enables the child to take an initiating role in social interactions from a very early age. Mutual attention and the subsequent communication between mother and child are important for later language development.

Snow (1989) also considers outcome measures in relation to the four special features of social interaction discussed above. She is not convinced that simple Mean Length of Utterance (MLU) measures are sufficiently sensitive to capture the effects of social interaction. She makes a plea for research efforts to be directed to measures of conversational skill, pragmatic skill and discourse skill—areas of language use often neglected, perhaps because of their complexity. Not only do we need to consider the social interaction antecedents of grammatical language, but we ought to be examining the consequences for the everyday social and communicative functions of language.

Child Interactive Speech

In the light of all the previous discussion, it seems that a more appropriate phrase to capture the mechanisms of reciprocity and inter-relatedness efficacious in encouraging language development might be child interactive speech. Although the role of the adult or more competent other may be initially to initiate and maintain the child's participation in conversation, the roles are flexible and certainly change as the child's language capabilities increase. The adult is regarded not only as the instigator and provider of isolated speech but as a conversational partner in an interaction in which the child is the other active participant. The adult uses simplified, modified language which capitalises on the child's propensity (possibly innate) to deal with and act on the input language (whether selectively or not is irrelevant here).

Mothers and other social participants encourage children from very early on by using vocal behaviours that mirror later language, attempting to communicate with their infants even before the infants are capable of communication (Snow, 1984). Furthermore, from the beginning of an infant's life, mothers in particular engage in face to face interaction with their child. It is claimed that these prototypical social interactions lay the basis for later conversational turn-taking patterns (e.g. Stern, Beebe, Jaffe & Bennett, 1977). In these early interactions, the mother is responding to her child, and this provides an additional, but extremely important, component to the language learning process (see Bohannon & Warren-Leubecker, 1985). As the child becomes a more active communicative conversational participant, the devices available for the establishment and maintenance of communication become more sophisticated, particularly on the child's part. Children move from proximity-seeking behaviours in the early months to more distal activities. These activities enhance the development of language by inviting a contribution from the mother—and she usually responds by talking. The nature of the language directed to the child varies in complexity, in linguistic function and in form depending on the child's developmental status, level of participation and role in the interaction. Such verbal initiations are the domain of the adult to begin with, although the child's complementary role is well established. Initiation of verbal exchanges signals the child's entry into social communicative interchanges. Child interactive speech thus encapsulates these notions, emphasises the fundamental importance of language as communication, and underscores the contribution both participants in social interaction make towards the child's language development.

In concluding this section on language spoken to children, it has become apparent that language development, instead of being regarded in a narrow sense as the acquisition of linguistic rules, involves the active engagement of the child and another communicative participant. Language is not simply the innate deduction of syntactic rules from the available language environment. Rather, language has become a system of syntax, semantics and pragmatics derived from social communication. Children are presumed to be innately predisposed to act on the language input, this input facilitating the development of language. The input, and the person providing the input, and the child who derives the output are at least equally important. None the less, the *process* of language development, *how* the child learns language, given the facilitatory nature of the input, has (quite rightfully, I maintain) become fundamental. Social interaction assists and facilitates the process of language development, and language itself assists and facilitates later social interaction. A narrow perspective of language does not do justice to the myriad language forms and functions a child must learn in order to become a linguistically competent and communicative member of the prevailing society and culture.

Child Constraints to Language Learning

In considering facilitatory mechanisms for language, it is worth noting that certain constraints also operate. These limit in important ways the amount and type of information infants and young children can deal with, despite a social environment conducive to maximise developmental options. There are two basic types of constraints that operate to restrict both the speed and the direction of a child's language acquisition. These restrictions may conversely be regarded as precursors to language. Firstly, from birth an infant must develop physiologically and neurologically and these developments include brain mechanisms as well as the auditory and articulatory mechanisms necessary to hear and produce all the complex sounds of language. Not unrelated to these developments are the cognitive constraints that operate to limit the child's ability to process language, both as input and output. Included in such cognitive limitations would be memory and general intellectual functions.

Physiological and neurological constraints are more pertinent in infancy when very young children are beginning to make sense of their environment. Studies of children's reactions to the acoustic properties of language spoken to them confirms the early ability to detect changes in pitch and other prosodic cues in speech. More recent work (e.g. Fernald & Kuhl, 1987; Hirsh-Pasek et al., 1987; Kemler Nelson, Hirsh-Pasek, Jusczyk & Cassidy, 1989) points to the infant's probably innate ability to orient to and distinguish aspects of adult speech that have communicative value, such as pauses on word or phrase boundaries rather than mid-word. This ability, while evident at quite young ages, lays the basis for later finer discriminations in the speech flow, all of which facilitate later speech. Speech perception studies, discussed at greater length in Chapter 3, demonstrate the ability of infants of under three months of age to distinguish between specific speech sounds. Again the ability to discriminate, for example, "pah" from "bah" has a facilitatory effect on later understanding and production of speech. Further physiological development, as well as better control over the aural equipment, both in terms of detection and localisation of sound, and increasingly fine distinctions in the speech flow being heard, enhance subsequent understanding of language.

Infants also produce vocalisations from an early age (see summary in Garton & Pratt, 1989), and further developments in the ability to produce sounds that increasingly approximate those in the adult language depend on the maturation of the vocal apparatus. Early vocal productions consist of vegetative noises and crying, followed by cooing and laughing. The earliest sounds produced (at least in English, possibly universally) are consonants produced at the front of the mouth, such as "p" and "t". Development then proceeds towards the back of the mouth to consonant sounds such as "k". Early vowel sounds produced include those made at the back of the mouth such as "a" and "ə" and development proceeds forward. Greater refinement is achieved both through greater articulatory control and increased use of aural feedback. Deaf children develop productive speech sounds normally until greater reliance on aural feedback is necessary for further progress, usually around the age of nine months. These children provide confirmatory evidence that initial vocal development is independent of aural feedback but that the development of more refined sound production is dependent on such auditory mechanisms.

Cognitive constraints to language development are more difficult to study partly because the question is usually addressed from the standpoint of examining the relationship between children's first words and cognitive development (see, for example, Gopnik, 1988). By tackling the issue from this perspective, it is usual to describe concomitant developments in language and cognition and discuss their inter-relationship. Thus, for example, Gopnik (1984; see also Gopnik & Meltzoff, 1984, 1987) documents a functional shift in the nature of children's language at the one-word stage, a shift she attributes to the development of certain specific cognitive abilities. A shift to the use of more "cognitive-relational" words seems to parallel a move into Piagetian Stage 6. Prior to the shift, language is used primarily in a social sense, to attract attention or to indicate people or objects. The child's major desire is to communicate socially. A movement into the more advanced cognitive level involving the co-ordination of means–end relationships marks a transition into more planned and thoughtful cognition, mirrored in the use of language. Language becomes more regulatory and involves such words as "gone" and "more", signalling complex relationships. Gopnik is cautious not to over-state the importance of the relationship between cognition and language, pointing out that from a very early age many functions of language are social and communicative, and that both language and cognitive development are mutually influential.

PARAMETER SETTING AND LEARNABILITY THEORY

As stated at the start of this chapter, parameter setting and learnability theory are currently in vogue in linguistics, and have clear ramifications for developmental psycholinguistics. Both derive from Chomsky's original transformational grammar theory of language, but both involve modifications to that theory. Both have begun to explore issues of language development, and learnability theory in particular relates to much of the recent research on child directed speech. The underlying premise of the innate predisposition of children to learn language remains, as does their tendency to act on the input language in some way. The other component, the output as manifested in (knowledge of) rules of the native language, also remains. What changes are some of the theoretical perspectives that explain and predict the proposed mechanisms for development.

Parameter Setting

Parameter setting is a specific example of a testable theoretical position that has been derived from Chomsky's theory. Because of the failure of transformational grammar to explain theoretically the development of language, it became apparent that what was needed was a theory that would encompass both the innate component in a broad sense as well as the specific role of experience in shaping the innate propensity for attaining language structures. Coupled with this, the output data from LAD were acknowledged as being only of positive instances of the target language. That is, correction is rarely offered for agrammatical language produced by children and hence they never receive feedback for incorrect syntax produced. This "no-negative evidence" hypothesis did not accord well with an acquisition system that purported to induce grammatical rules from the range of language heard and produced. Thus, instead of the previous conceptualisation of a LAD with a rule-writing system, parameter setting proposed the innate under-specification of linguistic rules. These rules then became more specific as the child was exposed to language. In other words, the value of the parameter is set but is open to resetting in the face of triggering data in the input language. (This is open to question as the parameter may have a neutral initial setting that is then "fixed" by triggering input data (Cook, 1988).) The child must actively use the language she encounters to specify the correct value for the parameter, or the correct specification for that linguistic rule in the particular speech community. It has been postulated that there are two assumptions that make the parameter setting model a successful predictor of language acquisition (Williams, 1987). These are that each parameter can be set independently of other parameters and that there is a restricted range of permissible values a parameter may have, each of which represents an intermediate grammar on the way to the achievement of what is termed by Chomsky knowledge of the principles of universal grammar, i.e. the linguistic competence and knowledge shared by all adult language users. However, it may be that these assumptions are false and refutable.

Developmental studies using a parameter setting model are still rather rare, and are also linguistically quite sophisticated rendering them incomprehensible to naive readers. The following account is an oversimplification of Hyams' (1986) study. Her study compared English-speaking and Italian children and their acquisition of the null subject principle. This is termed the "pro-drop" parameter. An example of the "pro-drop" parameter is (in Italian) "Vado al cinema stasera", translated as "(I) go to the movies tonight" (Hyams, 1987, p. 3). It was assumed that all grammatical sentences have subjects but that in pro-drop languages such as Italian, a lexical subject is optional even when the null subject can subsequently have definite pronominal reference. What is the initial setting of the parameter for pro-drop? This was Hyams' research question, which she explored in relation to the acquisition of Italian and English sentences. Her argument was that the early grammar of English was a pro-drop grammar and various triggering data induced the resetting of the initial parameter and accounted for the transition to the adult system. In her study of English-speaking children, she found subjectless sentences in their output. These were judged not to be a performance limitation nor connected with the syntactic complexity of the uttered sentences. In addition, subjectless sentences were more common than objectless sentences and the missing subjects were not semantically restricted, for example, to agents of action. The omission of a subject was hypothesised to be a consequence of the pro-drop parameter being set initially to require subjectless sentences. With time, the linguistic rule would be altered and the parameter reset to permit the use of a lexical subject in sentences. Hyams argues that in English the early grammar shifts from a pro-drop grammar to one that more closely approximates the adult language of English.

Parameter setting represents a relatively restrictive characterisation of the process by which the rules of language are learned. It is clearly different from the hypothesis-testing process proposed by the early LAD models of acquisition whereby rules and their application were generated and tested against a model of language conceived of as principles of universal grammar. Under-specified or even empty parameters are subject to determination or specification with exposure to language. It can further be argued that a parameter setting model accords well with a social interactionist perspective, since it is the child's active involvement with the language that permits the use of direct positive instances and indirect negative evidence (i.e. the child noticing that certain constructions do not appear in the input language) to trigger and set the innately determined parameters. According to Gleitman and Wanner (1982), parameter setting represents a realistic process that permits the acquisition of language to be governed by all the child's mental faculties and not only a linguistic one. It also permits dropping of the instantaneous requirement of the earlier acquisition model.

Learnability Theory

Learnability theory encompasses many of the notions incorporated in parameter setting and described above. It does however make some broad fundamental assumptions about the nature and course of language development, enabling its application over a wider range of research. Learnability theorists regard language acquisition as a logical problem (Atkinson, 1987). Learnability is thus a hypothesis about the logical mechanism(s) required for language development, both facilitatory and constraining. However the theory concurs with a social interactionist perspective, as it assumes the child herself is central to language development, constructively working on the input data, utilising a set of (under-specified) grammatical principles. The child is also equipped with a learning procedure which includes a defined end-point, in this case adult grammatical or linguistic knowledge.

Wexler and Culicover (1980) were among the first to specify what a theory of learnability would look like. Their major focus was on the learning of Chomskian transformational grammar, but the general principles have found applicability elsewhere. As stated at the start of the chapter, it is assumed there is a number of language hypotheses available to the child learner, there are data available to the child, the child has a (learning) procedure for selecting hypotheses and there is a criterion for learning. As in parameter setting, an induction model of language learning is proposed. The critical component is the learning procedure adopted by the child, and it is this aspect that has become the focus for developmental psycholinguists.

Integrating learnability theory with a social interactionist perspective involves the assumption that the language directed to young children plays some role in development. The learning procedure then can be examined as part of the child's involvement in social, communicative interactions. As noted previously, it has been difficult to prove that maternal speech adjustments *per se* have any facilitatory effects on language development. What they permit is for the child to discover or induce linguistic rules as and when the time is appropriate. Gleitman et al. (1984) remind us of the child's contribution to the learning process. The child acts on the input speech selectively, as he needs to or as he is ready. Any specific adjustments of their speech made by mothers seem to facilitate the child's restriction of viable hypotheses, or permissible settings for parameters (Gleitman & Wanner, 1988).

The learning procedure available to the child enables his interpretation and utilisation of linguistic information in relevant ways. Induction of linguistic rules happens because the child can link the linguistic input with his interpretation and understanding of the world. This, needless to say, alters with increased cognitive and linguistic capabilities. How the mapping actually occurs is open to debate (see, for example, Maratsos & Chalkley, 1980; Wexler & Culicover, 1980; Braine & Hardy, 1982). The details do not concern us here. What does seem important is that speech input, albeit in modified form, acts as a catalyst for the child learner, providing examples of grammatical speech that facilitate the induction of linguistic rules. In parallel, the mother interprets and imputes meaning onto the child's grammatical output, facilitating the mapping of form onto meaning in a culturally acceptable manner.

A testable learning or learnability hypothesis has been proposed recently by Keith Nelson (1987) who describes a "rare event learning mechanism" (RELM) that permits language development. RELM is a cognitive mechanism applicable to all symbolic systems, emphasising the close relationship between cognitive and linguistic development. "Rare events" are isolated moments of understanding of form-to-function mapping which initiate the acquisition process. There are four phases of acquisition: preparation, analysis, assessment and consolidation. While the model is in the early stages of development, it would need refinement to be adequately applicable to the acquisition of language, for example, where it has been argued that a social component is necessary. Although Nelson (1987) believes that RELM depends on the child's observation of the use of the communication system by experts, the child's processing mechanism is central. The social interactionist position could incorporate RELM as a within-child process of learnability, but in addition the mother's role as provider of linguistic input and interpreter and instantiator of output is vital.

Learnability theory assumes an innate predisposition on the child's part to learn language, by providing the child with broad parameters requiring fixing. This may be one of the driving forces behind the child's need to interact socially with members of the speech community and to make attempts to process and interpret language from an early age (see Hirsh-Pasek et al., 1987, for an example of infants' early awareness of prosody cues as syntactic markers). Social interaction provides the child with the vehicle to interpret and use language, to induce linguistic rules and to become a competent meaning-maker.

SUMMARY

This chapter has drawn together a range of studies which all illustrate how language input can influence the speed and direction of a child's language development. Starting with studies that examined how the grammatical forms used by mothers when talking to their children are then taken up and used by the children themselves, the research enterprise shifted focus to examine the impact of maternal speech on early semantic and pragmatic development. An expansion of maternal speech to include the conversational context of early language interchanges has broadened the scope of the research as well as producing compelling evidence for the facilitatory role of such interactions for language development. The phrase "child interactive speech" was coined to capture the joint responsibility of both conversational participants to promote the child's language development. The definition of language has likewise shifted over the short history of the research, starting from a narrow structural denotation where language was equated with grammar as construed by Chomsky to a more wide-ranging definition of language as communication. In this latter tradition, adult–child conversations (with or without recognisable linguistic forms) are the cornerstone for the development of linguistic rules, word meanings, the rules of conversation, as well as introducing and acculturating the child into current social conventions and expectations.

Parameter setting and learnability theory were discussed in terms of how linguistic input may directly or indirectly influence the child's learning of language. These models of language learning acknowledge the centrality of the child as an active processor and constructor of language. Linguistic rules are induced and modify or specify innately determined parameters. Active participation in the learning process makes parameter setting and learnability theories attractive as testable hypotheses about the interactive effects of the child with the language input.

An innate propensity to interact with other humans lays the foundation for later conversations. This propensity has refinements such as quite sophisticated communicative, visual and auditory abilities ready for use from birth. Infants can communicate from the moment there is someone there to interact with, by crying, moving in synchrony, by watching others, by localising and listening to sounds. All these abilities are precursors to becoming a competent conversationalist as well as a user of language. These abilities both facilitate and constrain social interaction from infancy, paving the way for entry into language.

CHAPTER THREE

Social Assistance and Language Development

Language is primarily a system of communication and in examining how children learn language, it is important to study how they come to learn to *use* language. The acquisition of language as a grammatical, or structural, system, it is argued, depends not only on innate predispositions but also on the inculcation of rules which permit the grammatically correct expression of the language. Part of this process depends on the active interaction of the child, from a very early age, with linguistically competent members of the same language community or culture. Indeed it has been argued (for example, Bruner, 1983; Garton & Pratt, 1989) that the acquisition process is facilitated by social interaction because of the assistance offered by the more competent partner in any social interaction. Adult assistance does not simply refer to an adult in an interaction whose mere presence encourages a child to learn. It implies some additional constructive aspect to the assistance which actually facilitates what the child learns and the learning process.

Social assistance has also been interpreted to imply aspects of the child's genetic endowment that predispose her to interact with other people. These forms of assistance are innate propensities or mechanisms that facilitate the establishment and maintenance of social relations and social interaction. This chapter will consider, in turn, forms of adult social assistance, and mechanisms of social assistance that exist prelinguistically, both specifically in relation to the development of language. The emphasis will be on the forms of adult assistance available and how these might assist in the creation of social conditions conducive to language use and development. The focus is on the potential forms and processes of assistance rather than on specific linguistic effects or outcomes as was the case in the previous chapter. In addition to considering explicitly recognisable forms of assistance that an adult might bring to bear on communicative interactions, some of the early social mechanisms available from infancy that might create and maintain communication are discussed.

FORMS OF ADULT ASSISTANCE

Scaffolding

Bruner (1977) and Cazden (1983) refer to one of the social facilitatory processes as "scaffolding". As a construct, it has been used not only in characterising language acquisition but also in children's problem solving (Wood, Bruner & Ross, 1976), where it is sometimes referred to as "contingent teaching" (Wood, 1988). Scaffolding is a metaphorical description of a teaching process that facilitates children's learning. This process is local, task-directed and focuses the child's attention on relevant aspects of the task. Scaffolding directs the child, via small understandable steps, to achieve success. Contingent teaching, or scaffolding, is derived from Vygotsky's "zone of proximal development", and is regarded as a means of ascertaining whether or not instruction is sensitive to the child's actual and potential levels of development. Wood (1988) outlines five instructional options that can be used to classify a mother's teaching level in a construction task with her child. These levels show a decrease in the amount of specificity in the instruction provided by the mother as the degree of responsibility taken by the child increases.

Cazden (1983) distinguishes between *vertical scaffolding* and *game-like routines*. Vertical scaffolding as characterised by Bruner is seen when adults, usually mothers, progressively demand more information from a child while maintaining the focus on the existing topic. For example, while reading a book, a child may spontaneously utter "spider". The mother has various options in the way she responds to this (and these options may further be dependent on whether the "spider" utterance was elicited or spontaneous—I have assumed the latter). She can respond by asking about the spider: "How many legs does the spider have?", which requires the child either to count, to approximate a count or for the mother to continue the interaction by facilitating the counting herself. Or, the mother may respond by asking "When did you see a spider in the garden?" requiring a recalled answer from the child, with possible continuation of the dialogue. The mother focuses the child's linguistic efforts on particular topics but continually demands new information or elaboration. The mother responds contingently to the language produced by the child, encouraging and instructing the child in its use. The mother is able to pace the child's linguistic progress and asks pertinent questions at a level appropriate to the child's own level of linguistic production and understanding. And the most curious thing about scaffolding in language development is that mothers (and others who spend a lot of time with very young children) respond intuitively. They require no training in contingent responding. Their knowledge of children and their capabilities at different ages guides their communication as well as the method of instruction selected (Wood, 1988).

Although it is believed that this scaffolded or contingent form of dialogue does not teach a child anything about grammar (Scollon & Scollon, 1979), it is crucial for the child to learn about communication. Turn taking, responding to questions, knowing how to answer—these are all aspects of dialogue that a child must learn both for future conversational competence and for later writing. More specifically, children are also learning about linguistically appropriate forms that can be used—for example, to answer questions—as well as the functions of words. Thus, to return to the above example of the spider, a child must learn to respond to different questions such as "How many legs does the spider have?" requiring a cardinal number, "When did you last see a spider?" requiring a temporal noun as a reply, or "What does a spider do?" requiring a verb in the reply. A mother can carefully prime and instruct her child to produce a syntactically and semantically appropriate response to her questions. While questions are one of the predominant linguistic forms noted in mother–child conversations (Wells, 1985a), other language forms and functions are used in interactions, particularly at home (see Tizard & Hughes, 1984). In addition, mothers talk about past and future events, they use language to control their children, to play with their children and to read to their children. These, and other similar contexts, provide opportunities for scaffolding to occur, for mothers to teach their children about how to use language.

As children begin to produce increasing amounts of language and also initiate conversations, a mother's teaching role does not stop. Rather it becomes more refined and adjusted to the child-initiated questions (of which there will be hundreds if not thousands!). While many of the responses will themselves be questions, mothers also elaborate on and extend both the child's knowledge base and the forms and functions of language available. Quite a proportion of these questions will be seeking clarification of the child's intended meaning, requiring the child to reiterate or rephrase her original statement or question. However, mothers will usually seek to maintain and extend the conversation and will use means to encourage communicative interaction. The processes whereby this occurs will be discussed later.

The other form of scaffolding, *game-like routines*, refers to structured interactions which themselves can provide the necessary contingencies and predictabilities for language to develop. A range of such interactions has been studied (see, for example, Garvey, 1984; Tizard & Hughes, 1984) and the nature of the support provided described. In games and other structured activities, the scaffolding is sequential, with the adult trying to utilise and maximise the available external structure and, by using the available slots and juncture points in the structure, push the child to her limits, very gently of course. The most specific study of the nature and role of game-like routines in the child's early acquisition of language can be found in Bruner's (1983) book in which he describes formats.

Formats

The communicative contexts within which language is mastered by the child, Bruner dubbed "formats". Formats encapsulate social regularities and encompass regular social events such as mealtimes, bathtime, going to the shops, playing "peekaboo" or reading a book. A format has a regular routinised structure and involves at least two people—the child language-learner being one. The child becomes familiar with the routine and the predictable language used either because it is a daily occurrence (mealtime, bathtime) or because an individualised game becomes so well known, it becomes stylised and routinised. According to Bruner (1983), not only are formats "nonnatural" and conventionalised routines, they are constitutive and idealised. In addition, they are rule-bound in the sense that there are underlying, implicit rules to each format, the realisation of which permits management of the format. Indeed, many adults capitalise on the rule-bound nature and the predictability of the structure to use the same language each time the game is played. An adult may expect the child first to enter the routine at appropriate designated entry points and then to produce the appropriate language, initially at the correct slots or juncture points only. Finally, the adult demands the correct form and function of language to be produced and the child to play an equal part in the interaction.

Bruner (1983) documents the development and role of formats in language acquisition. The emergence of language depends on the structural assistance provided by the social routines in which adults and children engage. Bruner illustrates the interdependence of language and the contexts of its use by describing first how structured games permit the child to learn about language. He also analyses the emergence of two linguistic entities—request and reference—in relation to the contexts of their appearance and development. Both of these are described below, first focusing on how formats assist in the acquisition of language—its form, its functions, and its use. Following this, the development of request is described.

Play and Language Bruner explains how one format—an appearance/disappearance or "peekaboo" game—with its elaborate, but unstated, structure, enables a young child to learn a great deal about language and communication. An analysis of the constituent structure of the game, and the permitted embellishments and deviations, shows how very young children first enter into the game and how, over many months, the child's role evolves. Bruner argues that fine-grained analysis of all the elements in such formats and games shows how children learn about the management of social interaction, even before linguistically appropriate forms are produced. The basic structure of the game, involving the disappearance and reappearance of an object or a person, the element of surprise and the reaction of the child, remains the same. A mother can vary these elements by, for example, altering the timing of the reappearance or varying the intensity of her "Boo!", while the fundamental structure remains invariant. The child learns at what point in the game she is allowed to vocalise, where she is permitted to take a turn and what the mother's management role is. The mother's language controls aspects of the game as well as assisting the child to participate in the action. Not only is the game conventionalised but the use of language is too, thus facilitating the child's linguistic development.

The scaffolding provided by both the game's structure and the mother's role is constitutive for the child's language development. As Bruner remarks (1983, p. 62), the constitutive nature of such games enables the child to understand sequences in the context of an ordered game. Language firstly accompanies the action, then precedes it, anticipating the action. The early vocalisations become richer and more linguistically "correct". Further, the sequential nature of the format provides a means for the child to learn about aspects of communication, such as turn taking, role negotiation and the consequences of action. Bruner argues that formats are powerful vehicles for the transformation of early communicative functions into linguistically sophisticated speech.

Requests   Formats need not only be stylised sequences of activities but can also refer to contextualised occurrences of language. In order to study linguistic requests, Bruner examined the emergence of three different request forms, identified as occurring in different contexts. *Object request* involves direct request of a visible object, initially proffered by another person. The requests then become directed to objects that are more remote spatially, and eventually to non-visible objects. *Invitational requests* are, as the name suggests, requests for another person to share in an activity. These are often conventionalised in that they appear in specific formats. Finally, *requests for supportive action* are those requests made by a child for an adult's assistance to achieve a particular goal. The adult assistance is generally strength or skill (to undo or untie something perhaps or help to stand up or reach something) at first, rather than knowledge. The role of the mother is different for each type of request and her expected response would vary. None the less, she is imposing culturally appropriate conditions in the way she complies with and responds to the child's requests.

Invitational requests are apparent in three obvious contexts, some of which are formats. First, an adult may be invited to do something such as read the child a book. Bruner (1983) termed this an asymmetrical request, in contrast to a parallel request where a child requests her mother to share an activity such as jointly watching the television. Thirdly, there are alternating invitational requests where a child requests her mother participate in a turn-taking routine such as the building up of a castle from blocks and the child knocking it over. This alternating sequence may continue over an extended period. All three forms of request were recorded contemporaneously in the transcripts analysed by Bruner and colleagues and none occurred more frequently than another.

Bruner observed that the language of invitational requests was more advanced than the language recorded for other requests. He believed this was due to their playful, non-threatening nature. Further, their predictability in terms of the expected adult response, meant their outcome was pleasurable, as well as rarely being refused. The linguistic forms themselves were initially vocalisations, becoming more refined and more specific over the child's first 18 months or so. Because of their invitational nature, these requests provide yet another way by which young children can learn about reciprocity in communication. They are learning about initiation of communicative interchange and the management of social interaction.

According to Bruner, in all cases regardless of whether we focus on the social, structural aspects of formats or on the emergence of a particular linguistic function, the principle is identical: The child's entry into the prevailing culture is via communicative interaction with another, more advanced, language user. Sympathetic and empathic scaffolding, namely, listening and responding to children's attempts to use language, coupled with the existence of culturally appropriate familiar contexts, are necessary ingredients for the development of a child's language.

Models

Models are another form of assistance adults can provide for language-learning children. They refer to grammatically meaningful language directed to children, often as a reaction to incorrect language. Thus there is explicit correction of a child's language, and the input received by the child is grammatically correct. From this model, a child is not expected to imitate directly the grammatical form. Rather, he is expected to learn from the adult's correct language use.

Cazden in her widely cited and seminal doctoral study (1965) explicitly compared modelling of language and expansion of children's utterances as means to encourage the development of language (specifically, grammar). She also included a control group of children who received no additional language input. Her major research question concerned the extent to which the environment might assist the development of grammar. In her original comparative study, Cazden found modelling to be less useful than expansions for the grammatical development of a small group of nursery school children. Expansions were relatively more successful because, it was suggested, they elaborated the child's own productive language and hence were more meaningful to the child. Modelling simply corrected the child's inappropriate use of language. However, it was acknowledged that neither form of environmental assistance impacted to an enormous extent on the child's grammatical development. Cazden (1988, pp.286-287), more than 20 years later, discusses why this may be so: "In hindsight, an explanation of the inconclusive results is that expansions and extensions [=modelling] can be functionally equivalent with respect to semantic complexity" (my clarification).

Some of the research on maternal speech to young children was stimulated by this initial lack of an effect of environmental assistance. Much of this research was discussed in Chapter 2. Other research has focused more on the types of grammatical speech to which children are exposed and the potential influence this has on their grammatical development. Semantically contingent speech (Snow, Perlmann & Nathan, 1987) includes speech related by meaning, by topic, and includes modelling and expansions. But it also includes a "latent shared representation function" (Cazden, 1988, p. 286), in that adults are presumed to be interpreting what is going on in the child's mind. That is, an adult interprets a child's language according to their knowledge of the child, knowledge of the child's linguistic capabilities and knowledge of the world in general. Whatever the basis, semantically contingent speech is functional for the child's learning of language. However, as pointed out in the previous chapter, semantic contingencies are paralleled by syntactic contingencies, since in adult–child speech there is a high degree of form-to-function mapping (Ninio & Snow, 1988). So by sharing meanings, adults and children also share linguistic forms. Separately or together, either might facilitate language development.

As should now be apparent, scaffolding and modelling are not independent forms of assistance. Both involve external assistance and both occur in adult–child conversations. The mechanisms responsible for language learning have not yet been defined, but there is little dispute that an environmental component is essential. It is necessary but not sufficient. In addition, an innate propensity to learn language is required, a tendency to interact and to communicate in the broadest sense. Children should be provided with as wide a range of linguistic forms and functions as possible, first in a limited range of contexts with maximal support and assistance. Less aid can be supplied as language development proceeds and contexts broaden, and children can use language more efficiently and effectively.

Direct Instruction

Direct instruction, as illustrated by Cazden (1983), refers to the explicit teaching of language and linguistic forms to young children. It is generally confined to the learning of social conventions such as "Hello", "Goodbye" and "Thank you". Such language use is considered polite. Direct instruction occurs when children are asked or told to comply with a request such as "Say 'Goodbye'". Indeed an amount of direct instruction is concerned with the teaching of social conventions like politeness, e.g. "Excuse me, are you using that pencil?", where the polite form is likely to guarantee a response (Garton & Pratt, 1990). Direct instruction may also relate to the teaching of assertion through verbal rather than physical means. So, children are taught to say "I would like to use that pencil", rather than pushing in and grabbing it.

Direct instruction is also noted however in didactic interactions where the express purpose is to teach the child something, often colour names or the numbers for counting. In these cases, the concept is introduced and the child encouraged to repeat the word and to understand its meaning. For example, a mother might show the child four red smarties and say "Look, four smarties. One, two, three, four.

There are four smarties. Can you say four?". The mother is inviting the child to repeat the word in a context where she believes she has clarified its meaning. It is also probably the case that the concepts selected by a mother for direct teaching are likely to be those valued by the particular culture in which the child is developing. In English-speaking cultures, as mentioned, colour words and number words are frequently taught since they are important discriminators. They are also educationally relevant. It thus makes sense for a child to accept invitations to learn language that is culturally conventionalised as it will form a part of the skills of communication needed for functioning in later life.

PREDISPOSITIONS FOR SOCIAL ASSISTANCE

In order for communication to occur between a child and another member of the cultural or social community in which she is developing, there must be some initiative or motivation. Humans seem destined from the outset to interact in a social way with other humans. Infants are equipped with innate abilities that are necessary for and enhance social interaction. There has been an enormous amount of research examining the early precursors to and possible prerequisites for language development. Most of these prelinguistic precursors take account of the social nature of the child and the functional value of some of the behaviours exhibited from birth. Many of these behaviours develop to assist entry into a social relationship with another person, to engage another person and to maintain social contact. Sensory systems such as vision, hearing, touch and smell all develop to permit increasingly refined social interaction. The vocal tract itself matures to enable articulation of an increased range of sounds. Some of these physiological, neurological and sensory developments are closely related to language development and may even have evolved to facilitate the acquisition of language. I will consider some of the more recent research on infant abilities that may assist the development of language, especially those abilities that are social in origin and in nature. Early entry into social relationships is beneficial in the short- and long-term because of the learning that results from interactions.

The Establishment of Prelinguistic Social Relationships

From the very moment of birth, social interaction takes place. Mothers are encouraged to handle and talk to their newborn infants and to establish a social relationship. The behaviours involved in the formation of a social relationship derive from various sources and have multiple outcomes. For example, the study of attachment (Bowlby, 1969) involves an examination of the importance of different close relationships for later healthy development. This view is closely aligned with Freud's psychoanalytic theory. Other areas investigated under the rubric of social development include emotional development and social or person perception (Bremner, 1988).

The establishment of social relationships prelinguistically is nowadays regarded as an interesting research topic both in its own right and as potential for describing and explaining later social, cognitive and linguistic developments. Social perception is a necessary component for the development of subsequent relationships. Various studies using different facial forms have shown that young infants can both recognise the human face (as opposed to faces with scrambled facial characteristics; for example, see Wilcox, 1969) and can distinguish between human faces. The ability to discriminate between one human person and another on the basis of their facial characteristics has been found in infants as young as two weeks (Carpenter, 1974). Although the research studies on social perception have not reached consensus on the earliest age at which infants can, firstly, recognise human faces and, secondly, discriminate between different human faces, partly because of methodological differences, all agree that the early manifestation of this ability suggests its importance. An infant must be able to distinguish the primary caregiver from, for example, a stranger. Basically, this makes sense for survival as the mother is the giver of food, warmth and protection.

On what bases infants make these judgements and discriminations we cannot be sure. They may be visual, as discussed above, they may be auditory—as infants have been found to be able to pick out their own mother's voice (DeCasper & Fifer, 1980)—or they may be linked to their sense of smell (Macfarlane, 1975). Bremner (1988) suggests that social perception may be multi-modal, involving integration of a range of sensory information. The more cues available, the easier the infant's task. Cross-modal integration allows for the possibility of information from one modality being used by or in conjunction with another modality. Further research is needed in this area of social perception before we can be sure whether person discrimination depends on single modal, multi-modal or cross-modal sensory integration.

As well as being equipped with sensory systems that facilitate the receipt, integration and storage of incoming information, infants have another means whereby they can establish social relationships. The concept of attachment as articulated by Bowlby (1969) involves a "motivational-behavioural control system that is preferentially responsive to a small number of familiar caregiving figures" (Bretherton, 1985, p. 3). Attachment, as the name suggests, involves the establishment of a relatively intense relationship between an infant and the mother or other caregiver. Because of its derivation from Freudian psychoanalytic theory, the concept of attachment has been well described and researched. According to the theory, normal adult personality can be traced back to progressions through a series of psychosexual stages of development. Abnormal personality reflects fixations at certain stages, when conflicts are unresolved. For example, at the oral stage the infant's mother is the preferred object of attachment and failure to form a satisfactory relationship leads to oral fixations. These are manifested in later life by nail biting, smoking and other more serious perversions involving the mouth. Social relations are important since according to attachment theory the mother provides the infant with her breast which supplies not only milk but allows for the formation of a dependent relationship. Withholding of the milk supply leads to frustration on the infant's part, which may affect her later personality development.

Attachment has been described by Bowlby (1977, p. 201) as "the propensity of human beings to make strong affectional bonds to particular others". Attachment theory also explains later emotional and personality disorders which can arise from separation and loss. Not only does psychoanalytic theory form a basis to attachment theory, but Bowlby incorporates aspects of ethological theory and control theory. Bowlby describes those behaviours characteristic of attachment theory, behaviours that serve to increase proximity between an infant and the primary caregiver. These behaviours are not related to feeding, sex or dependency, and while they are best described in the context of mother–infant interaction, they can be used to describe any form of attachment relationship. So, for example, it has been demonstrated more recently that infants can form multiple attachments, not only to their mother and father but to grandparents, caregivers and pets (Bretherton, 1985).

Social interaction plays a fundamental role in the development of attachment. The behaviours involved include both vocal (crying, calling) and non-vocal (ambulation towards mother, clinging) ones and many are manifested towards the end of the first year of life when the infant is separated from the object of attachment. Thus, a year-old infant may become extremely distressed when her mother leaves a room or when confronted by a stranger. Attachment theory can explain infants', children's and adolescents' distress and fearfulness when faced with unsettling or unnerving situations and their ability to cope with them, depending on the levels of security maintained from the attachment relationship established in the first year of life.

Part of the attachment bond is an emotional linkage between mother and infant. Social relationships are not simply based either on sensory perceptions or on the development of an attachment relationship, but some form of emotional development is occurring in the child. As Bremner (1988) points out, this is a neglected topic in infancy research, because it is extremely difficult to quantify the degree of warmth or to measure infantile sadness. Harris (1989) reviews some of the developmental studies of emotional expression in infants as evidenced in facial movements and expressions. Apparently discrete recognisable facial expressions of, for example, happiness, sadness, surprise, anger and disgust are produced by infants in appropriate situations (Izard et al., 1980). The origins of such facial expressions remain unclear—they may be innate or they may result from copying or imitating adults. Although there is clear evidence of facial expressions being used systematically, their specific meanings could feasibly be a result of interpretation by others. The innateness hypothesis has the strongest support from the empirical evidence, gathered from research on animals as well as infants and adults.

Emotion recognition has also been studied in infants. A study by Caron, Caron and Myers (1982) showed infants to be selective in what they look at when confronted with pictures of women expressing an emotion. Interest waned when the same emotion was portrayed but was enhanced when a different one was viewed, especially in the older, seven-month-old, infants. Again, it is not clear what interpretation infants make of different emotional expressions, other than by judging their behavioural reactions. Appropriate reactions do seem to predominate (Harris, 1989), lending further support to the innateness hypothesis.

The research on early emotional development has implications for the study of language development. Recognition of different emotional states suggests that infants are aware of gestures that play an important part in conversation. Research on non-verbal aspects of conversation (e.g. Wood, 1976) has shown that gestures made by the hands and the face play as crucial a role in normal conversation as the words themselves. Gestures convey emotional states as well as signalling turn-taking and indicating other conversational nuances. The development of a range of facial expressions to convey different emotional states also has value for later communication. Conveyance of happiness, sadness, surprise and disgust is often more forceful non-verbally. If the appropriate expressions are in the child's repertoire, then a foundation is formed for later conversations.

Prelinguistic Social Interaction

While the previous section focused on the establishment of early social relationships, this section now considers aspects of early social interaction that may be facilitative of language development. Relevant interaction skills apparent from early infancy include the synchrony of body movements with adult speech patterns, imitation of facial expressions and selective attention to aspects of speech (see Bremner, 1988, for further details).

Synchrony between an infant's movements and adult speech patterns was first described by Stern and colleagues (see, for example, Jaffe, Stern & Peery, 1973). They termed the synchrony noted between mothers and their infants as "conversational coupling". This primitive form of social interaction, which involves synchronicity between an infant's gaze to or away from the mother and the mother's vocalisations, was hypothesised to represent communication prior to speech. The regulation of gaze in a communicatively appropriate manner at a very early age (four months) serves a number of functions (Stern, 1974), particularly in spontaneous play. This early synchrony also extends to vocalisation (Stern, Jaffe, Beebe & Bennett, 1975), which was found to be integrated into communicative acts between mother and infant.

Stern, Spieker, and MacCain (1982) examined the acoustic properties of maternal speech that may facilitate infants' responsiveness (both non-verbally and verbally) to language. Specifically, it was noted that maternal speech to young children (or motherese, see Chapter 2) may be directed with exaggerated intonation and higher pitch and with variations in rhythm and timing compared to adult–adult speech. Again, further research is required to identify those unique characteristics of maternal speech to infants and then to investigate whether or not they are essential for the establishment and maintenance of social interactions and what role this acoustic information has for the child's language development.

So far, it has been argued that sensory information and the ability to form close emotional attachments to others are necessary for the development of social relationships, and further, that sensitivity to aspects of the speech flow is essential for the development of social interaction. What has not been considered has been the infant's ability (or inability) to integrate and co-ordinate all the various types of incoming information. Multi-modal integration of sensory information has been postulated as a possible solution to account for developments in the recognition and differentiation of human characteristics. Some of the auditory and perceptual mechanisms available for the infant to co-ordinate sensory input and to store this knowledge for future use have already been discussed. In this section I now wish to examine mechanisms (contingent ultimately on sensory input) that depend on social interaction for their functioning and, in addition, facilitate later social interaction. Meltzoff (e.g. 1981) proposes that infant imitation is an indication that incoming information has been stored as an abstract representation. Imitation of a previously executed action (such as tongue protrusion or mouth opening) indicates that infants, some as young as one or two weeks of age, can act on internal representations of perceptually absent actions.

The discovery by Meltzoff and Moore (1977) that infants could imitate perceptually absent actions not only challenged Piaget's widely-held theory regarding the role of imitation in cognitive development, but it provided evidence for the existence of an infantile representational system. And, by using sensory systems such as vision and motor systems, e.g. mouth movement, infants are showing evidence of integrating these. Further imitation studies by Meltzoff (e.g. 1981, 1983) extended the range of sensory systems to include touch and involved infants up to the age of one year. In all cases, there was evidence of sophisticated representational systems being used to store perceptually absent objects and actions. Meltzoff's series of studies provides compelling evidence for the infant having the ability and the representational means to benefit from all manner of interactional information. They are also evidence for the multi-modal integration of sensory information being an important means of dealing with environmental information. Sensory information need not be acted on immediately as the infant can act on stored representations. This latter very fundamental, possibly innate, ability is highly important for the development of later communication. It is also dependent on input from another social participant who provides the necessary information to act upon.

The regulation of early social interaction and communication between mothers and infants involves sensory and motor information to establish what Trevarthen (e.g. 1986) has termed *intersubjectivity*. Mutual communication, in its very broadest sense, involves the transmission of signals that regulate the interaction. These signals include body movements especially of the hands and head and verbal modulations (including intonation, rhythm and pitch changes). Also involved are the sensory systems of vision, audition, smell and touch which are moderated and governed by mental and representational processes. According to Trevarthen (1987, p. 3), these processes "cause humans to enter into harmonious and reciprocal states of consciousness and intentionality".

Drawing on a range of research, Trevarthen (1987) argues that from birth infants are equipped with an enormous range of behaviours to facilitate intersubjectivity. All those discussed above are included and Trevarthen develops a powerful developmental argument to account for the growth of a child's mental processes and her communication. Communication develops from birth, before language, and requires for its unfurling a cultural environment to support and enrich the inherited component. Mother–infant interaction is the vehicle whereby cultural transmission takes place, and infants are equipped with sensory, motor and mental means to achieve satisfactory interactions and transactions. Social interaction permits co-operation, communication and conversation in all domains and signals are transmitted between participants using a number of channels. Trevarthen has conducted a number of experiments over the past 15 years which demonstrate that a range of behaviours is available to very young infants for the initiation, re-initiation and regulation of communicative interchanges with their mothers (e.g. Trevarthen, 1977, 1987). Facial gestures, vocalisations and arm movements are but a few of the behaviours available and used from birth by infants for interactive purposes.

Rudimentary conversations (or "proto-conversations", Trevarthen, 1986) provide the context for the expression of various behaviours whose purpose and function become more refined as social conventions are learned, as new communicative behaviours become established, and as the child's mental and representational capacity increases. Learning is regarded as a social act whose very existence derives from social interaction—in particular, from intersubjectivity and joint consciousness. Innate predispositions towards communicative interaction assist learning, cognitive development and language development, realised via social interaction. And such interactions begin from the moment of birth, are culturally determined and are fundamental to subsequent development.

A further major factor in the developmental picture must also be the intentionality or the motivation of the child to communicate with another member of the prevailing culture. Communicative intent is the underlying principle in the development of social communication, with the implicit assumption that another person, usually portrayed as the mother, is an essential component of the interaction. The expression of communicative intent derives from both an innate need to interact socially as well as the interpretive role played by the other participant in the interaction.

Prelinguistic Vocal Interaction

Prelinguistically, infants produce recognisable speech sounds from around four months of age. Prior to this age, the vocalisations are predominantly crying, cooing and fussing sounds, as well as vegetative noises. Infant vocal production has been documented by Stark (1979, 1986), who traced the development of sound production in newborn infants until around the age of two years. The restricted range of vocalisations produced in infancy is partly due to the immaturity of the articulatory mechanisms both in the mouth and in the vocal tract (Sachs, 1985). This immaturity was discussed as a constraining mechanism in Chapter 2. Babbling, or the combination of various sounds, occurs usually around six months of age, coupled with pitch and intonation modulation. Some of the pitch and intonation variations resemble those of adults, and caregivers often respond as if infants have "asked" questions. The onset of babbling reflects increasing maturity of the oral cavity and vocal tract as well as control over the articulatory apparatus. Such control, implemented because of the use of auditory feedback, allows for further growth and refinement of the babbled vocal productions.

The relationship of prelinguistic vocalisations and later speech is complex and difficult to specify. Basically, the argument depends on whether it is believed that development is continuous (see, for example, Stark, 1986) or discontinuous (Jespersen, 1925). The widespread view that parents reinforced only those sounds that appeared in their native language (an argument put forward by Mowrer, 1954, for example) has largely been discredited. The most popular position today is that speech sound development is continuous with later speech development, this claim being based on careful longitudinal studies, meticulous data collection methods and careful documentation of the emerging sounds.

There is one final aspect of the developmental picture that requires consideration, which although slightly tangential to the main thrust of the assistance and interactionist argument so far, is sufficiently important for us to be reminded of its presence, namely prelinguistic auditory development and speech perception.

Prelinguistic Speech Perception and Auditory Development

Part of the process of participating in social interaction involves the increasing ability to hear the other person and, specifically, to interpret the speech flow. At its most basic, this means learning to discriminate between speech sounds as perceptual categories. This involves to a certain extent auditory development (both physiological and neurological) as well as the processing of linguistic communication and the two are usually considered together (Aslin, Pisoni & Jusczyk, 1983). The study of auditory development concerns itself with whether or not infants can hear at birth and, if not, when does a functional hearing system develop? Once a suitable age has been determined, the questions then become: What are the characteristics of such a system?; What is the sequence of development of auditory capabilities and sensitivities?; and What capacities are necessary for normal auditory development? (Aslin et al., 1983.) The detailed answers to these questions need not concern us here as our interest is in the role and function of social interaction in the development of communication. Examples of auditory development research include studies of infants' sensitivities to variations in intensity and frequency of sounds, studies of the aspects of acoustic information considered necessary for later development of speech perception and studies of anatomical and physiological changes occurring during the development of auditory functions. It is therefore important not to dismiss research on auditory development particularly as it relates, for example, to a child's developing capacity to distinguish differences in the intensity and frequency of speech sounds and to localise speech sounds accurately by head orientation. Both abilities assist in entry to and maintenance of social interaction, and these and other auditory perceptual skills are vital for language development. Such skills are further enhanced by age and experience.

As well as developing an increasing capacity to hear and discriminate sounds, infants also show evidence of rudimentary interpretation of the speech of adults. Speech perception research is clearly more pertinent to an examination of how social interaction can be of benefit to language development. For example, it has been shown that infants can distinguish speech as an acoustic signal from other sounds and respond to it differently (e.g. Liberman, Harris, Hoffman & Griffith, 1957). The ability to distinguish between two different phonemes better than between two equivalent acoustic signals (i.e. two identical phonemes) clearly has implications for processing of the spoken language. Such a skill has a functional value and has been reported as occurring from around two months of age depending on the acoustic property under investigation as well as the experimental methodology used.

Further studies have been conducted to investigate whether such discriminatory abilities are innate or not and whether the perceptual mechanism responsible is specialised for speech. The research studies have utilised innovative and imaginative techniques to tease out answers to these questions (for a full review, see Aslin et al., 1983). While all researchers agree that infants show remarkable perceptual abilities from an early age in a range of acoustic tasks, what has caused disagreement amongst them is the determination of what constitutes a perceptual category. Early research hypothesised that the phoneme, the minimum unit of language meaning, was the preferred category for segmentation of language. Consensus now favours the syllable-length unit of speech as being the infant's preferred minimum segmentation category. That is, infants show preferences for units of the speech flow that approximate a syllable (Aslin et al., 1983). Preferred segmentation is also noted for longer sequences of language, such as clauses (Hirsh-Pasek et al., 1987), providing additional support for the notion that infants innately segment speech in meaningful ways.

SOCIAL PROCESSES OF LANGUAGE DEVELOPMENT

How does language development take place? Are there social mechanisms that permit or expedite the development of language? Without being concerned with the specific means which different researchers have offered to account for the development of language, there are some underlying claims that subsume all such descriptive attempts. It has been assumed in the course of this chapter that there are two important components to social assistance. There is the rather obvious external social support offered by more experienced language users and there is an innate predisposition on the part of infants to interact socially. For this, they are equipped with a range of sensory and motor functions that facilitate social interaction from the moment of birth. These two components must be incorporated in one account.

There is a broad theoretical principle that can encompass all the accounts of the social mechanisms for language development. Intentionality, or the capacity to intend to mean, is an important issue in any examination of how infants learn, via social interaction, to communicate and converse. Does the infant *intend* to be understood, or *intend* to convey meaning, even prelinguistically? Compelling evidence has been brought to bear on this issue, particularly by researchers such as Lock (1980). Lock's argument, derived largely from Vygotsky's theory, is that from the outset, infants' communicative efforts (in whatever form) only exist and are given meaning because parents provide interpretations for these verbal and non-verbal activities. Adults impute intention to children's attempts to engage in interaction, and these interpretations have social significance as well as providing infants and children with relevant meaning to their behaviours. Lock develops his intentionality argument from an infant's preverbal period through to later language development, and focuses particularly on the process by which children's intentional communications become refined and language proper enters.

Although it is clear that many innate abilities assist infants to engage in social interaction, whether these are related to intentionality is a moot point. Instead it is therefore proposed that an adult responds to a child's early attempts to engage in social exchange, and in interpreting his non-linguistic communications then his linguistic approximations and utterances, imputes intention to the child. The adult assumes the child is intending to mean something by communicating, and interprets the behaviours (however primitive) accordingly. In so doing, the adult imposes the culturally conventional and acceptable meanings on the child's attempts to form social relationships and to engage in social interaction. Adults assume intentionality on the part of their child prelinguistically as well as linguistically. By imputing meaning to children's early utterances, they are assisting the child to map forms onto meaning as well as facilitating the learning of culturally appropriate conventional meanings. The adults' role in the interaction is thus two-fold. They assist or scaffold the child's rudimentary attempts to engage in social interaction. They interpret these efforts in culturally appropriate ways. They also talk to the child, providing language input to the child. This language represents a narrow range of form-to-function mapping from which the child comes to understand and use language. Further, when the child starts talking, the adult reacts to the productive language, possibly using the same simplified system of language forms and functions, while also imputing intention to the child. The child then internalises both the language used and the meaning imputed to it.

At a more fundamental level, it may be that by imputing intention the adult causes the child to become aware that intentions are conveyed between individuals. Unless this were the case (viz. an understanding of the communication of intentions via language), then there would be no point in a language system at all. The interactive nature of the mother–child conversation allows for the development of socially appropriate and linguistically correct language. The language acts to convey interpretations of intentionality as well as meaning. Whatever the precise mechanism, social interaction is the necessary component, as in communicative interchange with another person a child may begin to learn. Language becomes self-evident and necessary. This theoretical notion linking language, intentionality and communicative interchange will be reconciled in the final chapter with the perspectives discussed in relation to social interaction and cognitive development.

LONGER-TERM IMPACT OF EARLY SOCIAL ASSISTANCE

It is appropriate to conclude this chapter with a discussion of the longer-term impact of such early social interactions on language development. Most of the relevant research confirms the positive facilitatory effect on later language and literacy development of mothers communicating with their children from a very early age (Wells, 1987; Garton & Pratt, 1989). The form of communication usually studied is that of mothers reading or telling stories to their children (Garton & Pratt, 1989), as it has been shown that bookreading from an early age impacts both on spoken language development (Bruner, 1983) and on later accomplishments at school (Wells, 1987). Although the research has tended to examine the longer-term benefits of specific literacy activities noticed once a child begins school, the importance of the home in providing a stimulating language environment (bookreading and story-telling notwithstanding) cannot be understated (Tizard & Hughes, 1984).

Wells (for example, 1985b, 1987) discusses the impact of preschool literacy-related activities on later school activities such as reading and writing. In examining the effects on school attainment of a range of early language experiences, it is important to make a number of distinctions between the home as a learning environment and the school—often with the pre-school as an intermediary environment (see also Tizard & Hughes, 1984). At home, the mode of communication is (almost) entirely oral whereas, at school, reading and writing or written modes of communication are also emphasised. Indeed, one of the main functions of school, at least in the early primary years, is to teach both reading and writing. Writing (or written communication) is not missing from home life—for example, children paint and colour in and may learn to write their names, they go to the public library and they watch their mother write shopping lists (see Garton & Pratt, 1989, for a fuller discussion of this issue). Finally, at home, the mother and her child are often in a one-to-one situation where communication is easily directed to the other conversational partner. This is not the case at school, where a teacher may have a class of 30 pupils and can only communicate with them all at once. Individual interaction must be conducted at the exclusion of the others. This poses special communicative problems for the classroom teacher (see Pratt, 1985).

Wells (1985b) sought to investigate which home-based literacy-related activities were predictive of "success" at school. "Success" was defined as educational attainment on a range of literacy activities. He describes the shift from home to school as being from context-dependent learning to context-independent learning, a relative distinction created to characterise the differences between spoken and written communication as well as other differences, mainly to do with social class, that he discovered. Four different home-based activities were recorded specifically: looking at books or printed material; listening to a story; drawing/colouring; and writing. Some commonalities in these activities include the representation of information in a permanent form and the need for decoding of visual information or encoding of verbal information when going from one medium to the other. Looking at books was the most common of these activities and writing so rare as to be excluded from later analyses.

Two outcome measures were devised: a composite "knowledge of literacy" variable measured at age five and a reading comprehension score taken at age seven. Listening to a story being read was the only home-based literacy activity that was positively associated with both outcome measures. Although Wells acknowledges the limitations of the quantitative measures of pre-school literacy activities, he reports support for his hypothesis that early reading is likely to be facilitated by prior active engagement in being told or read stories. Listening to stories enhances an awareness of the context-independent properties of language, an awareness that greatly facilitates learning to read (and to write). However, the qualitative differences between the literacy experiences of children were far greater than any quantitative difference and Wells describes in detail differences in the extent to which children were exposed to the written word, the nature of that written word and the involvement of another active participant (often a parent) in the discovery of print.

Garton and Pratt (1989) and Wood (1988) highlight the different language demands of the classroom when compared to home. In both cases, the developments that take place at school are considered in relation not just to a child's experiences prior to school but also in relation to a child's continuing language development. Spoken language acquisition does not cease at the point of school entry when written language starts to develop more dramatically; rather, spoken language continues to develop, perhaps even into adolescence (Nippold, 1988). A range of linguistic devices continues to be acquired and existing language becomes more refined. In addition, children's vocabulary size increases throughout all the years of school and continues to be augmented during adulthood.

Many of the later language developments relate to the increasing need to produce sustained discourse. This is paralleled in the written mode by the expectation that children will write stories, requiring correct grammatical connectives ("and", "but") as well as internal cohesion. The language devices necessary for narrative cohesion are acquired relatively late, well into the school years (Karmiloff-Smith, 1986b) and appear first in spoken language. Children become increasingly able to conduct fluent conversations and to sustain topics of discourse either as a monologue or as part of a conversational interchange. During the early years of schooling, children are developing more sophisticated communicative resources, permitting the articulate and fluent expression of facts, ideas and fiction. These resources facilitate conversation with the teacher as well as being applicable to the written text. In fact, many stories that children are exposed to in the beginning years of school exploit such narrative techniques in their written form to maintain interest in the story. Children are thus exposed to conventional ways in which discourse cohesion can be maintained, such as connectives, the use of pronouns and determiners for intralinguistic reference and relative clauses. These devices, adopted from written sources, are then used by children when asked to relate a story verbally and when writing a story. Early exposure to such narrative structures, even in the home, must facilitate language learning, both spoken and written, in the school.

In conclusion, early social assistance with language development, coupled with exposure to a range of literacy activities, has longer-term benefits, especially when we consider the transition from home to school. A child who had the advantage of conversation with a supportive adult comes to school equipped with useful communicative skills that will permit fluent and articulate verbal interactions with their peers and teachers. Such children may also become proficient self-regulatory problem solvers (Wood, 1988; Garton, 1992). In addition, parents who have recited or told stories to their children (with or without supporting text) are providing their children with a valuable introduction to the language of writing with its more formal and cohesive structure. This too has been shown to have positive benefits on the primary school entrant, and presumably has longer-term implications. While spoken language is still incomplete in the early school years, much has been learned about both spoken and written language. Children who have received home conditions conducive to language development and have mastered verbal skills as well as knowing about the decontextualised language of the written word are advantaged as learners once they come to school. Such a privilege may be of life-long benefit.

CHAPTER FOUR

Social Explanations of Cognitive Development

PIAGET'S THEORY

The influence of Piaget's theory of cognitive development has been pervasive over the past 30 years. In Chapter 1, I outlined the tenets of the theory relevant for further elaboration in this chapter. Although Piaget was a keen watcher of children developing, his theory was by and large formulated without due respect to the social environment in which children develop. He was essentially concerned with the development of mental operations, conceptualised as internalised co-ordinations of actions. These operations allowed greater flexibility in thinking as children got older. Children's thinking progressed from being sensory-motor, i.e. driven by unco-ordinated perceptual and sensory systems, through pre-operational thought to fully operational thought whereby abstract mental operations such as reversibility (the ability to understand that an inverse action can cause the original physical or mental state to be regained) can be used on a range of materials. The pinnacle of development was formal-operational thought, attained in adolescence and characterised by inductive and hypothetico-deductive thinking. Piaget focused his theorising on (the acquisition of) scientific concepts, but acknowledged (Piaget, 1972) that these were not the sole domain where abstract thought was possible. The co-ordination of operations could be either internally or externally, i.e. socially, driven, and Piaget largely concentrated on the former, the endogenous mechanisms permitting cognitive growth.

Cognitive development was characterised as qualitative changes in thinking, changes that occurred as a result of the adaptation of existing cognitive structures. The child was considered to be an active constructor of her knowledge. Change was inevitable and irreversible, determined biologically, although the time required for change was permitted to vary from individual to individual, influenced by different levels of environmental stimulation. Piaget believed that the environment could play little role in the direction of the changes, only in their duration. It could provide general direction, not specific experiences to influence cognitive change. This view, of course, has not gone unchallenged (e.g. Donaldson, 1978; Wood, 1988; Grieve & Hughes, 1991). Piaget did counter some of his earlier critics although his theory of genetic epistemology remained intact, merely elaborated when disputed. At a more specific level, many of the observations and experiments conducted by Piaget throughout his productive and long life have laid the basis for modern developmental psychology. They have been replicated, refuted, disputed and upheld by researchers since the 1960s when the bulk of Piaget's works became accessible to the English-speaking world, after their translation. Only now in the 1990s, is there a slight dimming of his influence, particularly at the level of experimentation.

In addition to his relative neglect of the social environment, Piaget did not concern himself much with the role of language and communication in cognitive development. However, in one of his earliest books, he tackled the problems associated with the development of language (or speech) (Piaget, 1926), although his observations have not had wide appeal. Piaget tended to regard thinking and speaking as complementary processes within the child, rather than as potentially communicative. His descriptions of the development of language, including his observations of children's conversations, focused on the developing expression of clear and logical thinking and how young children were initially unable to take account of the other person in a conversation. Their speech was dubbed "egocentric", reflecting how they themselves viewed and interpreted the world, failing to take into account the other conversational partner. More advanced, or socialised, speech, involving amongst other things, arguments, make-believe and question asking, was a manifestation of more highly developed logical, or cognitive, structures. But again, early so-called socialised speech was centred on the self and was simply directed outwards. It was not social or communicative. Piaget's main concern was the explication of cognitive development and after his early foray into the realm of language, he barely touched on it again.

Piaget and Social Interaction

Of far greater relevance to this book are Piaget's views regarding the impact social interaction can have on children's cognitive development. Social interaction, specifically between peers, was postulated by Piaget (1932) as having a facilitatory effect on children's developing understanding of morality. In studying children's developing conceptions of morality, Piaget also examined how groups of children were able to solve moral problems collectively and in so doing advance cognitively. The kinds of moral problems that Piaget presented to the children were dilemmas where an accidental but serious outcome was compared with a deliberate but trivial outcome. The children's task was to determine the magnitude of the crimes and the relative culpability of the perpetrators. This research also bears on the issue of intentionality, as in order to judge the blameworthiness of the perpetrators, children need to be aware of the intentionality (accidental or deliberate) of the acts.

This research is best illustrated in an oft-cited example of Piaget's. In this dilemma, children have to determine who is naughtier: a boy who breaks one cup in the course of trying to obtain something prohibited from the larder or a boy who breaks many cups in the course of carrying out an activity requested of him. Younger (six- to seven-year old) subjects claim the latter child is naughtier because more cups were broken (this was termed objective responsibility by Piaget). Subjective responsibility, where the intent of the boy is taken into account (and here the fact that the first boy breaks a cup while being wilfully disobedient), is used as the basis for determining naughtiness by age nine or ten. Shultz (1980) has queried whether or not intentionality is really involved in these two moral dilemmas. However, the assessment of how children's intentionality or morality develops is not of concern here. More interest lies in the processes whereby children came to their solutions to the moral problems.

In the experiments conducted by Piaget, the children were placed in groups with like-aged peers. Discussion regarding the relative culpability of the two boys in the stories was allowed before a collectively agreed upon response was given. Piaget noticed that in these discussions conflict sometimes arose because children presented to each other different ways of viewing the problems and the outcomes. Such differing perspectives, arising from different (levels of) understanding, generated a need to convince both oneself and the other group participants of the correctness of the reasoning. As other children brought different points of view to bear, and different substantiation for their position, conflict or communicative argument would arise. A common solution to the moral dilemma was required and by the interpersonal discussion, children would be forced to adopt a single answer. Piaget argued that such interpersonal discussions and debate gave rise to cognitive growth, particularly in less advanced children. The most sophisticated position, justified with logical argument, would prevail. Its wholehearted adoption would ensure understanding by all the children.

The notion that interpersonal conflict is at the root of cognitive development finds support in other studies identified with Piaget. For example, the traditional three-mountains task, involving visual perspective taking, relies on a conflict between visual perspectives for the child to work out which is the correct photograph. Unawareness of the conflict between what can be seen by the child herself and what a doll positioned opposite (or at 90°) can see results in a young child always selecting a photograph of her own perspective. The young child does not experience a conflict between what he can see and what the doll can purportedly see. Once the child perceives the conflict and then begins to co-ordinate the various possible conflicting perspectives, a photograph depicting the doll's perspective of the three mountains is correctly selected. This process takes developmental time. Many studies have been undertaken to look at perspective-taking skills and their development (for a review, see Flavell, 1985): studies examining visual and social perspective taking, as well as studies of knowledge states or knowing what another person knows or does not know, studies of children's lying where the intent is to deceive the other person, and social cognition research which examines the awareness of social characteristics of others. In all cases conflict generated either between subjects or within the subject herself forces a reconsideration of one's own perspective before its adoption or rejection in favour of another. Typically, the final position is more advanced cognitively than that held previously. Both (or either) interindividual and intraindividual conflict can bring about cognitive growth.

While in general imitation fares poorly as an explanatory social mechanism for cognitive development, Azmitia and Perlmutter (1989) argue that in fact social facilitatory mechanisms vary with development and very young children, for example, may learn more through imitation than through the discussion of conflicting ideas since they lack the skills to conflict productively. This, however, does not take into account the process of interaction, within which conflict or imitation may arise. Social interaction can take many forms and its utility may depend on the extent of the partnership achieved, the type of task involved, the experimenter's expectations and goals, as much as the age of the child. Conflict should be regarded as part of the content of the interaction, not as a characteristic of the interaction itself.

In Piagetian terms, conflict is used to describe the process of social interaction that engenders cognitive growth and is usually operationalised as the overt expression (either verbal or non-verbal) of different perspectives. None the less, interactions themselves become characterised as conflict, especially in the experimental domain when conflict is engineered between participants. Regarding conflict as part of the content of the interaction shifts the focus away from the behaviours that manifest conflict to the way conflict becomes overt and resolved. Focus moves to the processes of the interaction, of which communication between participants is crucial. Without communication there could be no conflict, no disagreement, no agreement, no negotiation and no resolution. The communicative aspect of conflict has been largely neglected in the Piagetian inspired research literature except for an acknowledgement that it takes place. However, a consideration of the relationship between conflict in cognitive development and communication permits an examination of studies that find greater explanatory adequacy in Vygotsky's theoretical constructs. A description of relevant research and a proposed reconciliation between these two major areas of research is contained in Chapter 5.

In addition to interindividual conflict being essential for cognitive growth, intraindividual conflicts, which despite not containing a communication component, also bring about cognitive growth (Inhelder, Sinclair & Bovet, 1974). I shall focus almost exclusively on interindividual conflicts as mechanisms of cognitive development and scant attention will be paid to intraindividual conflicts. Nevertheless, conflict as a mechanism for cognitive change has been compared with agreement. In such studies (e.g. Bryant, 1982; Chambers, 1990), conflict is regarded as disagreement between opposing perspectives, either expressed between children or from an intraindividual clash of visual, spatial or strategic perspectives. Agreement occurs when perspectives or strategies are congruent and achieve the same end or result. Which is the more efficacious?

Bryant (1982) argues that children learn when strategies (producing a solution to a problem) agree rather than when they conflict. Conflict, he continues, tells a child something is awry but does not specify *what* is wrong nor how to adopt a correct strategy. On the other hand, if two strategies each consistently produce the same solution, then the child can be sure they are right. In general, the relative success of conflict vs. agreement for influencing the correct solution to a problem would seem to depend on the nature of the task involved and the experimental design used to test and compare cognitive strategies (Bryant, 1982; Karmiloff-Smith, 1984; Chambers, 1990). Consequently, the studies included in this chapter are those that have adopted a Piagetian definition of conflict (conflict as a process of interaction, or socio-cognitive conflict) and examined how cognitive conflict via social interaction facilitates cognitive growth.

In addition to the studies of socio-cognitive conflict, research on the facilitatory effects of the experimental context *per se* will be described. The developmental psychology experiment is itself a form of social interaction, and changing some of the components and processes of the experimental context has led to different competencies (often more advanced than previously claimed) in children being reported. Such alterations include the language used by the experimenter, the intentionality of the experimenter, the social relations inherent in both the experimenter–child relationship and the experimental materials and finally, in Chapter 5, the involvement of children unable to use conventional spoken language (in this case hearing-impaired children). It is also important to consider briefly the influence, if any, Piaget's theory has had on research on social aspects of infant cognitive development. What follows therefore is an interesting unfolding of an experimental tradition, aimed ultimately at explaining how children acquire and maintain knowledge.

Early Cognitive Development

Developmental research, informed by Piaget's theory, has been extensive and thorough. Conventionally, cognitive development is regarded as progressing through the sensory-motor period with the infant acquiring more refined motor, perceptual and social skills (see Harris, 1983, and Bremner, 1988, for reviews). Fundamental to the growth of knowledge is the development of the object concept, which culminates in the 18- to 24-month-old child being able to represent the locations and displacements of objects. Achieving the object concept is the goal of early development and requires the co-ordination of both motor and sensory acts. These acts develop from simple reflexes through to complex sensory-motor adaptations and constructions. Mental representation of objects is the final point of the development of sensory-motor intelligence. There is objective knowledge and understanding which permits subsequent intelligent behaviour, including the development of social relations.

Despite an enormous amount of research in early cognitive development, according to a Piagetian interpretation of development it is not until children have achieved mental representation that they are cognitively ready to participate in social relationships. Thus, any accomplishments during infancy are independent of social interaction. All the research that Piaget discusses where there is an acknowledgement of the social realm occurs *after* the sensory-motor period. Consequently, research influenced by Piaget's theory and focusing on the role of social interaction in cognitive development is research with older children, typically starting with children who are between three and four years of age. In contrast to the work on language development, there is a dearth of research that examines social interaction and cognitive development in the period of infancy.

This lack of research is not simply the outcome of Piaget's theory, but more fundamentally reflects the fact that most studies of cognitive development, in particular the object concept, depend on the child's ability to communicate. Generally, cognitive abilities are gauged by experiments in which children have to talk, or, at the very least, understand the language spoken to them. However, it has been claimed that early cognitive abilities, such as those described by Piaget, are not dependent on language, and are instead regarded as precursors to language and other representational activities. That is not to say there is *no* research, and the work of Gopnik and Meltzoff (e.g. 1987) examines the relationship between cognitive accomplishments and the use of language, albeit at the end of the sensory-motor period. Other research, also after the emergence of language, includes that of Sugarman (1984) on how children co-ordinate interactions with objects, interactions with people and, more complexly, object–people interactions, and research conducted by Pea (1980) on the relationship between the functions of linguistic negation and cognitive complexity.

A promising avenue of research is that described by Durkin et al. (1986), which although conducted with older children, employed a longitudinal language acquisition study to investigate early counting behaviour and number acquisition. Early mother–child interactions were videotaped and scrutinised for the emergence of a range of cognitive behaviours. The facilitative role of the mother in the development of such abilities could be examined. This may be a possible area for future research, although operationalising many of the later emerging cognitive behaviours in infancy may be the stumbling block that has caused the lack of research in this domain so far.

SOCIAL INTERACTION, COGNITIVE CONFLICT AND COGNITIVE GROWTH

Social Facilitation of Cognitive Development

The earliest studies that examined the influence of social variables on children's cognitive development considered performance on the conservation task as a function of membership of a group. The rationale for the efficacy (and superiority) of group over individual problem solving derived both from Piaget and from social psychology (Silverman & Stone, 1972). The research on group problem solving is vast but focuses on the behaviour of the group members or the outcome of the group discussion versus individual decisions (cf. the "shift-to-risk" described by Stoner, in Brown, 1970, or studies of conformity in Asch, 1956). The subject population in these early social psychology experiments tended to be adults rather than children.

The studies conducted in the early 1970s on group problem solving had several new characteristics. Not only did they extend the social psychological domain to include children, but the studies utilised tasks devised by Piaget to examine cognitive development. In addition, because Piaget's theory and experimentation were available in English, researchers became interested in the relevance of the ideas for education. More specifically, educational researchers were interested in how cognitive concepts such as conservation could be taught, how cognitive abilities could be enhanced and whether or not educational problems required new cognitive abilities. Teaching can be regarded as a particular type of group process. Thus, the experimentation involved marrying a paradigm from adult social psychology with a task from the developmental domain.

Silverman and Stone (1972) undertook one of the pioneering studies of the modification of cognitive functioning in young children as a result of group participation. They used the Piagetian conservation task (four versions of conservation of area) and pretested third-grade children (aged around eight years). On the basis of the pretests, children were classified as conservers, nonconservers or transitional conservers. Pairs composed of a conserver and a nonconserver were formed and were told of the difference in their answers on two of the pretest tasks. They were told to agree on one answer for each. Posttesting a month later was undertaken with both the children who had engaged in social interaction and a control group of non-interaction children.

During the interaction, it was found that the conserver's judgement prevailed in 11 out of 14 pairs. In yielding to the conserver's position, the nonconserver was noted to adopt the conserver's justification. On posttests, 11 nonconservers (from the same interaction pairings as mentioned previously) were reclassified as conservers compared to only one such shift in the control group. The success of the interaction sequence was attributable, firstly, to the fact that the interaction exposed the nonconserver to a verbal algorithm or model as the justifications adopted were the same as those communicated by the conservers. This possible explanation received support from other experimentation. Secondly, social exposure to a conserver may itself be sufficient to induce conservation. However, long-term effects of changes in the nonconservers' responses and their understanding of conservation were recorded in posttesting undertaken later by a new experimenter. In these sessions, there was 100% transfer of conservation responses to the new tasks which, although having different configurations, were soluble by the same rule. Therefore, this second explanation seemed unlikely to account for the long-term maintenance and generalisability of the conservation responses, and was discounted. Thirdly, the provision of a conflicting verbal model in the interaction may act as a catalyst for the acquisition of a conservation response in a nonconserver. This seemed the most promising explanation, worthy of more study. The robustness of the newly acquired concept of conservation was intriguing to Silverman and Stone, although the precise mechanism responsible still required further investigation.

Murray (1972), in a study contemporary with the one above, examined the acquisition of conservation through social interaction. His study was driven solely by Piaget's theory and the notion of conflicting points of view. Linking nonconservation to an inability to adopt another's point of view or role, Murray reasoned that confronting a child with opposing perspectives in the conservation task would induce a higher stage of thought. This he examined in two experiments in which six-and-a-half-year-old children were firstly pretested on a standardised series of conservation experiments. In the second session, one conserver was grouped with two nonconservers to work on the same problems as before, only this time agreement on an answer was required. Discussion and explanation were encouraged. One week later, individual assessment was undertaken with a parallel form of the standardised material used in the first two sessions. Two identical experiments were conducted to check on the robustness of the results.

Children classified as conservers had to have given at least one acceptable justification for a conservation response. However, conservers justified 75% or more of their correct responses, whereas nonconservers gave few if any justifications. After conflict interaction, there was an enormous shift of the nonconservers to become conservers in both the original and in the replication experiment. Not only was there a significant shift in the numbers, but the mean number of correct conservation responses also increased markedly. Interestingly, after conflict, the mean scores of the conservers also increased. No sex differences were recorded.

Murray (1972, p. 4) claims the data indicate strongly that social conflict is an "important mediator of cognitive growth". Social conflict not only assisted the cognitively less advanced children to make gains, but the conservers' performances were also enhanced. Like Silverman

and Stone (1972), Murray considers the social mechanism responsible
for the change (and for the maintenance and generalisation of change)
to be elusive and hence it is unspecified. Murray prefers the acquisition
of an algorithm or rule as an explanatory device for the progress,
especially in the generalisation tasks, although the role of
communication is not fully ruled out. The social nature of the interaction
quite clearly has a role to play, but its precise specification is not
formulated.

Silverman and Geiringer (1973) adopt more overtly a Piagetian model
in a subsequent study examining the influence of dyadic interaction on
the development of conservation. They were concerned with the concept
of "equilibration" which can be identified with the stable self-regulatory
processes in cognitive development. In Piaget's model, there is a stable
equilibrium which, when disturbed by mental restructuring, advances
to a higher stage of cognitive development. Equilibration can thus
explain the sequential nature of cognitive growth, and in this sense, was
the theoretical construct adopted. This study aimed to extend the
original study in two ways—one, to a younger age group and, two, to try
to examine in more detail the actual process of the interaction sequence
that caused the cognitive change. Finally, the maintenance and
generalisability of newly acquired conservation responses were
scrutinised more closely. Acknowledgement was given both to their own
earlier study and to the study by Murray.

A similar design to that employed by Silverman and Stone was used,
namely, a conservation pretest to determine levels of conservation, an
interaction sequence where one nonconserver was placed with a
conserver and the pair asked to agree on one single answer to a problem
to which each had previously given a different response. Posttesting was
undertaken by a second experimenter one month after the interaction
sequence. A control group was also included.

Out of the 23 pairs of subjects formed for the experiment, conservers'
judgements prevailed in 13 pairs on the two problems discussed. In
addition, two groups of children were identified—yielders, who
capitulated to the answer of the other child, and non-yielders, whose
conservation responses prevailed. Fifteen communication categories
were created, of which only eight were usable for analysis of the
interaction sequences. However, the distribution of language used
across the categories did not reveal any significant differences between
conservers and nonconservers, nor between yielders and non-yielders.
On posttests, nonconservers who yielded to the conservers' judgement
in the interaction sequence showed most progress across all tasks given.

Silverman and Geiringer claim this study convincingly supports
Piaget's equilibration model (as they define it) since nonconservers

yielded more frequently to conservers than vice versa, and those nonconservers demonstrated they had grasped the conservation concept in the posttest phase. In addition, the few conservers who yielded in the interaction sequence regained their conservation response during the posttesting. These results are taken as evidence against a social-learning model of conservation acquisition, although again the authors avoid making any firm commitment about the actual process mechanisms involved. An equilibration model assumes endogenous development with a non-specific role for the social environment, but discussion on this issue is overlooked.

John Murray (1974) explicitly examined social learning, or modelling, as a possible mechanism for cognitive development. He attempted to reconcile Piaget's views on imitation with social learning theory. Piaget believed that imitation will only succeed if the child has developed the necessary mental structures and operations to assimilate the model. Social learning theory, on the other hand, predicts imitation to be successful because it is a social, not a cognitive, activity. Conservers, partial conservers and nonconservers were classified after pretesting on conservation of substance tasks. Children were aged between five and ten years and the conservation classifications were both quantitative (number of tasks correct) and qualitative (taking the justification into account). In the intervening phase, the children viewed a videotape of either a conserving, nonconserving or partial conserving model (the same child played all three) working on a conservation of weight task. The training given was quite extensive, involving viewing four test trials and two initial equivalence trials. Children in each of the three classifications were randomly assigned to each of the videotapes. Posttesting evaluated children's performance on all the tasks used and seen.

Although not truly interactional, in the sense that children had no "hands-on" exposure to the materials and the communication, the complexity of the design ensured a thorough examination of the stability or otherwise of levels of conservation. The ability to conserve was highly related to age, but post-modelling performance was related to initial conservation status *and* type of model viewed. For example, children who viewed a nonconserving model tended to remain in their initial classification category rather than either advancing or regressing. Children who viewed a conserving model tended to progress, especially the transitional children. It appeared that modelling was most effective only when it was "in a developmentally sensible direction" (Murray, 1974, p. 157). Thus initial cognitive level was the clearest predictor of the effectiveness of modelling. Murray believes this result does not concur exactly with social-learning theory, although any discrepancy may be due to the way in which the study was conducted since it is not usual to study imitation of a developmentally regressive model. Both Piaget's notions of equilibration and social learning theory can partially explain the cognitive changes noted in the children in Murray's study, but again, close specification of the potential mechanisms involved was left unstated.

It was not until a study by Botvin and Murray (1975) that a comparison between social conflict (as studied by Silverman and Geiringer) and modelling was conducted. Botvin and Murray sought to compare the relative efficacy (in terms of performance on a conservation task) of, what they termed, active social interaction and passive social interaction. Active social interaction involved the actual confrontation of three nonconservers by two conservers, thus creating potential conflict, whereas passive social interaction involved the observation of both conservers and nonconservers responding to conservation problems. Both nonconservers and conservers were identified on a series of conservation pretests, the nonconservers being first-grade children (median age 6;9) and the conservers, second-grade children (median age 7;11). The nonconservers were assigned to one of two experimental intervention groups or a control group. In the social interaction intervention, two nonconservers were confronted by three conservers and all were instructed to agree on an answer to six conservation tasks. The experimenter performed the transformation of the materials and encouraged responding and justifications. Consensus had to be attained before another problem was presented. In the social modelling intervention, nonconservers in pairs watched the experimenter question each child in each social interaction group. The actual group discussion was not observed. All nonconservers were posttested on all the conservation tasks given in the pretest.

On the posttests, the social interaction and modelling children performed significantly better than the control group of nonconservers. However, the two forms of intervention were equally successful in inducing conservation as adjudged by posttest scores. Pre- to posttest gains in conservation responses were noted for both the social interaction group and the modelling group, but not for the control group. Furthermore, qualitatively, children progressed as evidenced by the appropriate justifications being used for conservation.

Yet again, however, these researchers lament that "it is not clear what the nonconservers learned in the interaction and modeling conditions" (Botvin & Murray, 1975, p. 798). Whatever was acquired can be gained by either active or passive participation in social interaction. Simple imitation seemingly cannot account for the progress since non-imitated justifications were recorded. None the less, the most parsimonious explanation offered by Botvin and Murray was that social conflict *is* successful due to imitation rather than exposure to repeated communication conflicts. The latter explanation is attributable to Piaget, but Botvin and Murray could find no reason to accept this. Rather, the exposure to a model, and moreover, a child model, is sufficient to induce cognitive change. Yet again, there is a somewhat unsatisfactory discussion and we are left pondering the important causal mechanisms involved. All researchers apparently agree that there must be specifiable mechanisms, that any such mechanism must become apparent in the course of either active or passive interaction, but it does not seem dependent on the communication or verbal conflict itself. It is however undoubtedly social and definitely leads to cognitive change.

Finally, two studies by Miller and colleagues (Miller & Brownell, 1975; Miller, Brownell & Zukier, 1977) examined the notion of cognitive certainty in young children. Children who have attained conservation, for example, are remarkably resistant to change, and the extent to which they hold this concept, often in the face of fierce opposition, was examined in a series of experiments. Social pressure, in the form of a nonconserving, conflicting peer, was induced via an interaction sequence. The robustness of the conserver's belief during the interaction was examined. Certainty was measured by a range of methods in the two studies.

In all cases, the conserver's answers to the cognitive problems prevailed and whichever assessment method was used, the operational children expressed greater certainty in their beliefs. Miller and Brownell (1975) discuss the role of peer interaction in relation to the yielding of the nonconserver and claim the superiority is definitely a cognitive rather than a social one. Conservers seemed to be more certain, express themselves more confidently and assert their views. They were also able to provide a range of acceptable explanations for their beliefs. In contrast, the nonconservers were qualitatively and quantitatively different communicators. Miller and Brownell do not discuss the implications of this result, at least not in terms of the link between the role of communication in the process of the interaction and the goal of the interaction.

Socio-cognitive Conflict

After the initial studies conducted in the 1970s, the emphasis altered and there was a bifurcation in the research. One strand of research continued to examine the ways in which conservation (or whatever cognitive concept) could be made more attainable. This could involve training children in aspects of the task considered relevant in the manner of the research tradition begun by, for example, Wallach and Sprott (1964), Wallach, Wall and Anderson (1967) and Roll (1970), or could involve making alterations to the task so that it was more conducive to young children. The social aspects of this research will be considered later in this chapter. The other strand of research began to focus more directly on the interactional processes that might be pertinent for cognitive growth and stemmed from work conducted in Geneva by the social psychologist Doise and his colleagues.

The original research that Doise carried out examined the types of social interaction that might induce changes in cognitive, or operational, structures. Based on Piaget's claims that group judgements by adults or children often produce cognitively superior performances, Doise studied a range of collective decision-making interactions. In one study, for example, Doise, Mugny and Perret-Clermont (1975) compared the individual and group performances of five- to six-year-old children on a variant of Piaget's three-mountains task. This task requires spatial and visual perspective taking. A construction task was used requiring children to build model houses on a board. The buildings had to be located in accordance with a small-scale model, but with the base board turned through 90°. The location and orientation of the houses built by the children can thus be measured. This task can have a myriad of quantifiable variables and variants and can be used successfully with individual children, pairs and groups. (See Fig. 4.1 for a schematic diagram of the subjects' base board plus possible models in different orientations.) Children worked either individually or in pairs and it was found that the performance of the pairs of children was better, especially with the more difficult models.

In hypothesising the reason for this superior performance, Doise et al. (1975) dismiss any artefactual explanations concerning the superiority of one member of the pair, additive effects or imitation by the cognitively less advanced children. The preferred explanation, supported by other studies, e.g. Doise and Mugny (1975), was that cognitive operations are created during social interaction in advance of them developing in an individual. This enhanced cognitive level was further displayed in subsequent individual posttesting.

This research dovetails neatly with the earlier research but invokes a different explanation for the improved group performances. Enhanced cognitive functioning was not simply a result of the social interaction. Individual cognitive restructuring has also taken place. To determine the nature and extent of this cognitive restructuring, Doise and his colleagues have relied not only on the cognitive gains manifested, but also on the use of novel justifications by the children. The reason why

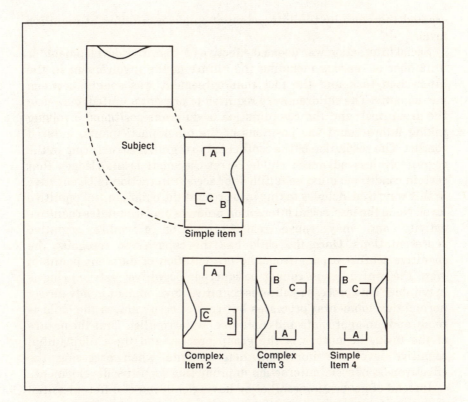

FIG. 4.1 Orientation of base boards for spatial construction task (Doise and Mugny, 1984).

the conservation task and other concrete-operational tasks have frequently been used in studies of peer interaction is because they offer the opportunity to study both cognitive gains and the explanations used by the children to justify their answers. Perret-Clermont (1980) convincingly demonstrated that originally nonconserving children who showed cognitive gain after social interaction were not simply imitating the other child. Novel justifications, other than those used in the interaction session, were recorded in the individual posttests, which also tapped generalisation skills, another manifestation of cognitive gain.

The studies conducted by Perret-Clermont typically involved an individual pretest, an interaction session where two conservers were grouped with a nonconserver and a generalisation posttest. She then compared the cognitive levels of children from the pretest to the posttest as well as analysing the different justifications used. Varying groupings were employed for the interaction sequences, but the basic experimental procedure remained the same throughout. Cognitive conflict was created therefore by the interaction of children of different cognitive levels.

Social interaction was deemed effective for cognitive development for a number of reasons including the nature of the involvement in the interaction task and the fact that agreement was sought between participants. The children were required to present a united answer to the group task and the co-ordination of different positions, involving taking into account the positions of the other participants, induced conflict. The resolution of the conflict led to cognitive structuring in the cognitively less advanced child. Perret-Clermont acknowledges that certain conditions must be fulfilled for social interaction to be effective in this way; this includes taking into account the child's initial cognitive level. None the less, social interaction prompts and stimulates cognitive activity and may cause restructuring of a child's cognitive representations. Once the child has the capacity to recognise the cognitive conflict arising from the presentation of different points of view, the contradiction cannot be ignored. Cognitive restructuring is inevitable. This process facilitates cognitive development in advance of normal developmental processes but cannot occur unless the child is ready and can appreciate and capitalise on the conflict. Thus the nature of the task, the nature of the group process and the child's initial cognitive level are important determinants when assessing the effectiveness of social interaction in promoting cognitive development.

Instead of generating conflict by having children of different initial cognitive levels working together to solve a concrete-operational task, Doise and Mugny (1984) undertook a series of experiments in which cognitive conflict was generated by different means. Like Perret-Clermont, they adopted a post-Piagetian perspective on cognitive development and explored in depth the nature of socio-cognitive conflict and how it might facilitate cognitive development. Different social situations were created and conflict induced. Examples of the social interaction sequences used include the "co-operative game", in which children require social co-ordination. A number of pulleys require co-ordination in order to move a central part attached by strings to the pulleys along a predetermined path. In another task, Doise and Mugny explored further the co-ordination of spatial perspectives via the reconstruction of a model village as described previously.

In all cases, and by whatever means conflict was generated, social interaction produced superior performances on the tasks used. As discussed by both Perret-Clermont (1980) and Light (1983), certain social and task conditions must prevail for the interaction to be effective. Asymmetrical social relations, appropriateness of the task selected (in terms of the potential for conflict, solubility and inherent attractiveness for children to complete) and the generation of conflict are all necessary but not sufficient for cognitive progress. Interaction with both the social world and the non-social world is important for intellectual development. New cognitive processes are created and advanced through social interaction. Specifically, socio-cognitive conflict is needed for cognitive restructuring. Doise and Mugny (1984) propose a theoretical model to account for cognitive development in which there are mutually interactive and spiral paths of causality between the social and cognitive domains.

The Genevan studies prompted a number of other investigators to research the necessary social conditions for cognitive development. Typically researchers seek to enhance the cognitive abilities of the less advanced (by virtue of age or cognitive level or both) participant in the interaction. Pairs are formed of children with different cognitive levels, the assumption being that the less advanced child will develop cognitively as a result of being presented with a conflict. This conflict is usually but not always composed of an opposing but correct perspective on or solution to a cognitive task. Light (1983, p. 72) claims that the solutions need not be correct as two partners, for example, can both be "equally wrong". Confrontation with a different solution can prompt cognitive restructuring. So, some researchers have conducted studies using pairs of children of differing abilities and, in some cases, where neither child possesses the actual cognitive ability in question.

Ames and Murray (1982) reasoned that, if social conflict is necessary for cognitive growth, nonconservers should benefit equally from being exposed to correct conservation and from other (incorrect) nonconservation judgements. In their study, young children between six and seven years were provided with information that conflicted with their nonconservation judgements. The conflict conditions studied by Ames and Murray were social interaction between peers, modelling by a peer, pretence (where the child had to pretend the opposite of what he thought before), non-peer conflict (where the conflict was induced by the experimenter transforming the material), and a control condition. They argued, on the basis of the success of the social interaction condition relative to the other experimental conditions, that conflict, even where the information is incorrect, is more important than exposure to the correct solution in promoting subsequent cognitive development.

Glachan and Light (1982) paired children who initially adopted different strategies to solve a problem. Like Ames and Murray, they found that in order for cognitive growth to occur, the children had to be able to resolve the conflict generated in the interaction. Merely watching the correct solution did not cause cognitive growth. For cognitive development or advancement, children had to be actively involved in the conflict, be permitted to talk about possible solutions and to engage in the practical actions needed to solve the problem correctly. The conflict need not be between the "right" and "wrong" answers; rather, the child must be allowed the opportunity to resolve the conflict generated or induced, for development to take place.

Light and Glachan (1985) explored further the notion that the opportunity to resolve the conflict is the important function of peer interaction. They used a task which they believed was more verbal so that actual progress could be monitored during the task and measured. They also included 12-year-old children in one of their studies. Children of all ages were advantaged cognitively by working together on the cognitive tasks, irrespective of the task or the mode of presentation (one of the tasks was presented by computer). The task eliciting greater amounts of verbal communication enabled an examination of the relationship between the verbal interaction and cognitive development. None the less, cognitive advancement was also recorded in the less verbally demanding task. Unfortunately, Light and Glachan (1985, p. 223) do not pursue further the relationship between communication and cognitive development. Instead they conclude that "Profitable interaction may ... take different forms in different task environments", and then go on to discuss some of the educational implications of their results.

Social Marking

Before concluding this section on cognitive conflict and social interaction, it is worth considering the research on social marking. This research combines children's conceptions of social reality and their cognitive development. Social marking refers to the social meaningfulness of a cognitive task as construed by the developing child and can be regarded as analogous to social representation. Doise and Mugny (1984, p. 30) discuss social marking in terms of " ... the causal intervention of social regulations as norms in cognitive development". By this they mean there is a direct correspondence between the relationships amongst social participants in an interaction and the cognitive relations inherent in objects that mediate the interaction. Thus, in any interaction, the social relationship between the participants is governed by implicit and explicit social conventions or norms. Doise and Mugny claim this relationship is mirrored in the cognitive relationships between the characteristics of objects in that situation. For example, the unequal status of adult and child in an experiment may mediate (either facilitate or hinder) the cognitive relationships in the task itself. Doise and Mugny further believe that social markers may sometimes be essential in socio-cognitive conflict interactions because new cognitive structures may develop to create and maintain the social organisation.

To study social marking experimentally Doise and Mugny arranged a correspondence between the models used for construction in the usual experimental set-up and the accepted structure of adult–child relations. Thus instead of the usual houses and other buildings to be constructed around a central reference point, say a swimming pool, they utilised a schoolteacher's desk as the central reference point and substituted school desks for the houses. They claim there exist, *a priori*, necessary social relations in these materials based on children's relationships with their teacher. Copying the model onto a spatially transformed board while retaining the correct relative spatial locations should, it was hypothesised, create socio-cognitive conflict. The asymmetrical social relations portrayed in distinct spatial relationships should further encourage conflict.

The procedure used was similar to the one used by Doise and his colleagues in other studies (see Doise & Mugny, 1984) and the results indicated that social marking conditions produce greater cognitive benefits in the posttest conditions both for children working as individuals and for those working in groups compared to the conditions involving regular materials. The effect was particularly strong for children who participated in group work with socially marked materials. For the individual, the conflict was generated in the social marking condition by a contradiction in the operations that are required to complete the task and the social norms that usually govern the situation. Even this form of conflict produced superior posttest performances. The teacher–child relationship as depicted spatially is difficult to ignore and the conflict so induced causes cognitive restructuring. The overriding conclusion to this and other such studies by Doise and Mugny is again a reminder that not all social interaction promotes cognitive development. While Perret-Clermont urged care in the specification of the necessary components in the interaction that cause cognitive development, she highlights the child's initial cognitive level as important. According to Doise and Mugny, we need also take into account the social nature (including language and communication) of these interactions as the critical variable in the development of cognition.

COGNITIVE TASKS AS SOCIAL INTERACTION

An extension of the claims made for the success of social marking as a facilitatory process is that modification of the social conditions may enhance children's performance on cognitive tasks. Thus, if social interaction is indeed crucial for children's cognitive development, then it could be expected that performance on Piagetian-type experiments of, for example, conservation and class inclusion would be facilitated simply by the experiment being intrinsically a social "event". And indeed, modification of the social parameters of tasks designed to measure cognitive development has usually led to improved performance by young children. As a rule, the tasks used in experiments of cognitive development involve a child interacting with an adult, who asks the child questions pertaining to a display of experimental materials. An assessment is made of a child's cognitive level and, on the basis of tests carried out on many children of different ages, a developmental sequence is proposed. Rather than children being tested before and after intervention (either individual or group), children participate in a single experiment, with another person. Donaldson (1978), on the basis of results from a number of experiments, questioned whether this represents a valid way of assessing children's cognitive competence. I shall draw on the work concerned with the development of conservation, as this not only provides continuity with the socio-cognitive research, but also represents the research with most breadth.

The assumption that the experimenter–child interaction is a typical assessment procedure that can influence the child's performance in some way led researchers to examine what changes in the context would induce apparent improved performance on these cognitive tasks. Some of these changes have involved the nature of the social interaction and others have involved other social variants. Studies that involve changing the nature of the social interaction include those in which modifications of the verbal interchange between experimenter and child have produced dramatic increases in the number of correct conservation responses in children. Rose and Blank (1974) asked children the standard conservation question, namely "Are there more X here, more X here or are they the same (number, length or whatever)?", only once, after the materials had been transformed. Usually the question is asked twice, before and after transformation, thereby creating the (false) belief in the child that the materials had somehow altered and so further questioning was required. A changed answer would therefore be appropriate to this repeated questioning. In Rose and Blank's experiment, the single questioning was found to give rise to more conservation responses than in the standard, two-question conservation task. The elimination of the first occasion of questioning, pre-transformation, provided a more legitimate reason for asking the question post-transformation. Hence more children responded correctly. This result has subsequently been replicated and extended by Samuel and Bryant (1984) and Porpodas (1987).

McGarrigle and Donaldson (1975) altered social expectations in the experimental task in order to examine children's understanding of the conservation problem. Instead of the transformation of the materials being a visible and deliberate action, it was achieved accidentally, in full view of the child, by a "naughty teddy" whose sole purpose was to disrupt the "game". Even though the teddy was manipulated by the adult experimenter, a greater number of conserving responses was achieved than under normal testing conditions. It was claimed that having teddy accidentally transform the materials avoided the potential ambiguity between the experimenter's actions and her verbal references. For example, in conservation of number, the actions transform the materials along one dimension such as length or density whereas the verbal questioning makes reference to number. Having teddy "mess up" the experimental materials legitimises the experimenter's number questions. Like the studies in which only one question was asked, this study attempts to make sense of the task for the child. This was deemed to have been accomplished by the increased number of conservation responses from children younger than the expected age for conservation.

The study by McGarrigle and Donaldson has been extended and replicated (e.g. Light, Buckingham & Robbins, 1979; Dockrell, Campbell & Neilson, 1980; Donaldson, 1982; Hargreaves, Molloy & Pratt, 1982), although the mechanisms ultimately responsible for the increased success remain elusive and debatable (e.g. Neilson, Dockrell & McKechnie, 1983; Donaldson, 1983; Pratt, 1988). Gold (1987) believes that all these studies demonstrate an experimenter error and that increased success on modified tasks is explicable by Piagetian theory. Gold explains that closer analysis of Piaget's theoretical concerns is warranted by all those who embark on conservation-like experiments, and that the theory can more than adequately account for the differential success rates across modified tasks. None the less, most of the studies demonstrate that conservation abilities do appear at an earlier age than previously shown under standard presentations, but most do not offer a theory as to *how* this happens.

Further studies in this genre are discussed in Light and Perret-Clermont (1989). They conclude that while such alterations (or "discourse cues" as they refer to them) to the conservation task can have a large impact on the child's interpretation of the situation, they do not necessarily mean the child has fully grasped the concept of conservation. Undoubtedly these modifications enable some of the possibly dormant cognitive abilities to be tapped at an earlier age than was previously the case. This then has implications for educational processes (Donaldson, Grieve & Pratt, 1983). One important offshoot is that researchers are focusing increasingly on the developmental experiment as a social "event" (cf. Bronfenbrenner, 1973) which enables us to examine how the processes of social interaction affect assessment of children's cognitive abilities and the subsequent assumptions made about intellectual development.

A possibility, discussed by Pratt (1988), is that children who can conserve have not only attained an important cognitive ability but do indeed have a greater awareness of the nature and the purpose of the experimental situation. In his study, children individually participated in a standard conservation experiment in the morning. A second adult sat in the room reading a newspaper. In the afternoon, each child was interrogated by the second adult on the pretext of her not having paid attention in the morning and requiring to have kept a note of the proceedings. This provided a legitimate excuse for asking the children about the conservation task (and engendered some admonitions from the children).

After allowing the children to give a general description of the task, the second adult concentrated on two specific aspects, namely, the role of the experimenter and why she had been asking them all the questions. Many of the conservers made explicit reference to the experimenter's function as an assessor of knowledge. These same children could provide an accurate description of the reason for the transformation during the experiment. On the basis of these results and support from studies like Perner, Leekam and Wimmer (1984), Pratt argues for a link between the ability to conserve (liquid) and the ability to represent knowledge states of self and others, or metarepresentation. To understand why an experimenter is asking questions and to make inferences about their behaviours on the basis of this, requires second-order representational abilities (Perner & Wimmer, 1985), and perhaps such abilities are necessary also for the appearance of cognitive abilities. Notice, however, that for this to be manifested some form of social interaction must take place. Assessment of the knowledge state of a person requires the existence of another person who interacts verbally with the child. Social interaction may again be the essential catalyst in this process.

VYGOTSKY—THE MAN AND HIS THEORY

If *conflict* was regarded as the major mechanism for cognitive development according to Piagetian and post-Piagetian theory, then *collaboration* would be a correct descriptor for the developmental mechanism proposed by Vygotsky. However, this oversimplifies the broader vision of development described by Vygotsky (1962, 1978) and elaborated on by, for example, Wertsch (1985a). To anchor the theory and its impact more firmly, it is useful to digress and discuss some of the important historical, cultural and social influences that helped Vygotsky mould his position. It is also important to outline those theoretical concepts that have themselves influenced contemporary psychological research, particularly on the development of language and cognition.

Vygotsky's theory of development, as described briefly in Chapter 1, rests on the fundamental assumption that cognitive development does not occur in isolation. This means that cognitive development co-occurs with language development, social development and even physical development. Not only does the individual develop in all domains contemporaneously, these developments occur in a social and cultural context that cannot be ignored. This holistic approach focuses attention on the importance of taking into account all facets of an individual's development, including the broader social, historical, cultural, even economic, factors that contribute to an individual's competence.

In addition to regarding the child's development in its social and cultural context, Vygotsky's theory claims that cognitive and language development are explicable and comprehensible only by reference to these contexts. That is, the processes of mental growth depend on and acknowledge social contexts and influences. The word "processes" is essential to an understanding of Vygotsky's theory (1978, p. 64) and is explicitly recognised as such: " ... we need to concentrate not on the product of development but on the very *processes* by which higher forms are established. These processes are social in origin and in nature, and are peculiarly human".

Vygotsky's genetic analysis of human development has recently been described by Wertsch (1985a) who traces the theoretical roots of the genetic method. Wertsch (1985a, p. 48) summarises Vygotsky's view of ontogenetic development in terms of "the relationship between natural and cultural forces". By this he means that by and large Vygotsky perceived mental development as resulting from contact with social influences: a unidirectional transformation. The natural development of the child is deeply related to socio-cultural-historical forces. How individual, natural, development is transformed by social influences is best illustrated by research that has claimed to examine the movement, in young children, to mediational functioning in problem solving. Mediators required for successful problem solving include both language (or speech) and practical intelligence. Both will be discussed below after consideration of Vygotsky's methods of data collection.

As well as influencing Vygotsky's theory, an ontogenetic orientation also informs his research methodology. Concerned to study human development as it occurred within its natural environment, Vygotsky examined both normal and abnormal developments in children. None the less, he maintained a doggedly single hypothesis, namely that the social environment influences individual development, and not vice versa. Vygotsky, according to the critique of Wertsch (1985a), failed to take into account the impact the individual can have on socio-historical and cultural contexts, themselves constantly changing. Indeed, Vygotsky's research was more limited—he dwelt almost entirely on how the acquisition and deployment of mediational systems such as spoken and written language result in cognitive advancement. And it is precisely this aspect of the research work that has such importance and force in the 1990s.

Vygotsky's genetic research method involved either the study of naturally occurring changes or the impact of social changes on the individual (e.g. Vygotsky and Luria's study of the impact of social restructuring, including the provision of formal education, in Uzbekistan on an individual's psychological (i.e. cognitive and linguistic) levels of functioning—Luria, 1976). Naturally occurring individual developments studied included the development of writing (Vygotsky, 1978) and the development of speech (Vygotsky, 1962, 1986). In addition, the former was examined by providing materials in advance of the child's capabilities and witnessing the outcome. What *does* happen when a toddler is given a pencil and a sheet of paper?

The experimental method was also utilised by Vygotsky, but in keeping with his theoretical perspective, children were often "tested" in problem-solving situations where additional information or contextual support was provided. The purpose of these experiments was to examine developmental changes in relation to the extent to which the environmental aids were used and the extent to which they assisted in the solution of the cognitive problem. As a way of obtaining diverse and rich data, such an experimental method has much to commend it but design or statistical analyses, which today are regarded as essential to any potentially publishable research study, were not paramount. Thus, controls were not adopted or adhered to in these experiments but instead a range of experiences and activities was observed and the impact of these on the child's developing cognitive strategies documented. In many ways, there is a similarity with some of Piaget's observations and early experimentation. Vygotsky however did not focus on the accomplishment of the goal or the solution; rather he was interested in how the goal was achieved.

Occasionally Vygotsky introduced obstacles to the attainment of the goal in order to study the cognitive resources and strategies adopted by the child to fulfil the task requirements. Rather inventively, these included pairing children with other children who did not speak the same language (they were either hearing-impaired or spoke a foreign language). This flexible approach to experimentation is also noted in many of the psychological researchers influenced by Vygotsky, including such luminaries as Luria.

Mediation, or indirect mediated activity, is, according to Vygotsky (1978), after Hegel and Marx, characteristic of human cognition. It refers to the internalisation of socio-historical and cultural activities and behaviours and is solely the domain of humans. Mediation includes both tool use and sign use, and signifies their coalescence. Tool use represents externally oriented behaviour while sign use, particularly language use, is internally oriented. The combination of tool use and sign use is uniquely human and permits the development of higher psychological or mental functions. Tool use is equated by Vygotsky with practical intelligence, the latter term emphasising the linkage of tools to intellectual or cognitive development.

Practical Intelligence as a Mediator

Mediational functioning refers to the use of decontextualised, but culturally conventionalised, signs such as language, to facilitate solving a problem. It is usually characterised by a shift from the use of concrete "aids" to assist in the solution of a problem to more abstract methods, including language. These mediational techniques facilitate goal-directed thinking, permitting planning, monitoring and achievement of problem solving. Vygotsky described the shift from reliance on concrete assistance to more abstract forms of problem solving as the transformation of practical activity. However, he construed language (=speech) as developing independently of practical activity, at least in the early phases of development. In Vygotsky's opinion (1978, p. 24) their convergence marks "the most significant moment in the course of intellectual development ..."

According to Vygotsky, in the preverbal period of development, children's tool use is akin to that of monkeys and apes. Once speech (and any other sign system) is incorporated into an activity that was once the domain of tool use, the action is transformed along new lines. Language enables the transformation of the behaviour into more abstract realisations, permitting the more flexible mental activities characteristic of humans. The dual origin of sign systems versus practical activity is the hallmark of Vygotsky's theory, and the most important theoretical contribution made by him was the unification of two processes. In particular, speech was accorded an organising function that both facilitates tool use *and* permits the transformation into new and higher forms of intelligent behaviour.

Practical activity is epitomised by the infant or the child mastering their environment and is evident from birth. To achieve any goal, for example for an infant to focus on the mother's face or, later, to grab a rattle, requires specific actions. These actions are determined partly by the infant's physiological and neurological development as well as by her mastery of specific actions or behaviours. Children master increasingly complex behaviours including perception and sensory and motor movements, which enable more flexible and creative ways of accomplishing activities.

Specifically human forms of tool use, or practical activity, are difficult to find. Vygotsky addresses this issue from the inverse perspective and claims, after Köhler, that apes are unable to develop and use even elementary sign or symbol systems. (This may be disputed nowadays with the wealth of research showing advanced symbol and sign manipulation in chimps (for a summary, see Berko-Gleason, 1985), plus evidence showing an awareness in chimps of the existence of a "theory of mind", e.g. Premack & Woodruff, 1978, and relevant chapters in Whiten, 1991.) Vygotsky reiterated the folly of researchers tackling the study of practical intelligence independent of the study of language. The two aspects can inform the development of intelligence or mental processes. Before examining how Vygotsky approached the conjoining of speech and practical activity, it is important to describe how he viewed the development of language.

Language and other sign systems are culturally constructed domains. Number and language systems are communicated to children from early childhood. The children then transform and act on that system, using it to mediate their cognitive activities. Using language in particular assists a child to attain goals successfully, either directly through verbal self-monitoring or indirectly via asking another person for guidance (which in turn may be given directly or indirectly). Many recent studies claim to find evidence of mediational functioning in very young children (often in counting or arithmetical tasks, e.g. Gelman & Gallistel, 1978; Saxe, Gearhart & Guberman, 1984; Saxe, Guberman & Gearhart, 1987). Although young children can use and manipulate a range of mediational systems, it is not clear if they are incorporating the knowledge into their cognitive functioning. Saxe et al. (1984) conceived of number as a culturally constructed system, in the same vein as Vygotsky construed any sign system. Their study, which involved mothers instructing their two-and-a-half to five-year-old children to match numbers, examined the interweaving of cultural goals (as communicated by the mother) and the child's shifting developmental goals. The level of instruction provided by the mothers varied as they adjusted the goal structure of the task in accordance with the child's level of functioning, both at the macro level (chronological age) and the micro level (task difficulty increasing across the session). From the instructional directives issued by the mothers, 11 goals and sub-goals were identified ranging from the mother providing a direct cardinal representation of the model for the child to match ("There are three Xs here. Go and find three Ys"), through to the mother providing only the overall goal to the task ("Get the same number ... "). Saxe et al. (1984) found that there was negotiation of the goal structure within the interaction as well as according to the child's ability level, as determined from pre-testing, and the child's age. Mothers adjust the task (i.e. their construction of the perceived difficulty of the task) according to the needs of their child and the children adjust their own goal-directed behaviour according to the instructions provided by the adult.

Saxe et al. (1987) extended their earlier study to examine the relationship between social class and numerical competence in young children of preschool age. Numerical understanding was hypothesised to be related to numerical environment as operationalised by everyday number activities and the nature of social activities involving number. One of the primary aims of this study was to examine children's "goal-directed adaptations" (Saxe et al., 1987, p. 4) to their numerical environment. Children's generation of numerical goals was examined as was the shifting sociocultural organisation of their numerical environment. As the research is published as a monograph and consequently a number of studies is reported, I will extract only the overall conclusion regarding the social and developmental processes involved in children's numerical activities and understandings. Many of the findings, in addition, were related to social class, itself a determinant of available numerical environment, with four-year-old children from middle-class homes displaying greater numerical competence in complex problems.

Although embracing Vygotsky's broad theoretical principles, Saxe et al. (1987) claim to have integrated a study of the developmental shifts in children's goal-directed activities with a cultural analysis of children's numerical activities. Negotiation between mothers and their children regarding the organisation of culturally determined activities (such as number) is again highlighted. Children's experiences with number, they claim, are not pre-existing in the minds of the mother or the child; they are the product of a negotiation process. Mothers adjust their goal-directed activities to the child's level of understanding and previous accomplishments. Number, itself a culturally determined sign system, is learned through a rich variety of numerical experiences provided and negotiated by the mother.

Studies such as these provide good evidence for the social construction of sign systems. It is thus easy to conclude that children learning these mediational systems are apparently incorporating them into their cognitive functioning. Mothers certainly adapt their directives (in a hierarchical fashion) with children's increasing age, their increased familiarity with the context, and prior success. They are assuming learning has taken place. Rogoff (1987) in her critique of Saxe et al. (1987) mentions this as a possible limitation of their research programme. The effectiveness of social interaction on children's learning and development has not been proved. The research has merely shown how the child's contribution to the interaction influences the mother's conception of the task and its goals which in turn affects the way she conveys her cultural understanding of number. Number and language systems have cultural value and it is important these values are transmitted. The contexts wherein number and language (and other sign systems) can be learned are created by mothers, although the process adopted is calibrated to the child's actual and potential levels of ability and understanding. Rogoff (1987, p. 156) talks of "guided participation" to include both the mother's role and the child's role in social interaction. Social and developmental processes are interwoven, and both the mother and the child have a contribution to make in assisting a child to learn.

Language and Speech

Vygotsky's account of the development of language rests on the premise that speech becomes increasingly decontextualised. It is also based on the notion that the development of higher levels of intellectual functioning depends on more abstract language. Abstract, decontextualised language enables more flexible conceptual thought. This contrasts, and is often confused, with the increasing tendency for egocentric speech to become more contextualised and specific. Wertsch (1985a) describes and compares the two forms of language—social speech and egocentric speech—and claims each form complements the other and both are necessary for development.

Egocentric speech is the language used to control and regulate behaviour and does not reflect egocentric thinking as Piaget (1926) would have us believe. For Vygotsky, egocentric speech is derivative from social speech and represents language used to mediate actions. Egocentric speech then becomes what is termed inner speech, speech unintelligible to others but which serves to regulate one's own actions and behaviours. Thus, language develops from the social dimension (language as communication) through egocentric language (largely intelligible language used explicitly to guide and monitor behaviour) to inner speech. Inner speech also reflects decreasing dependence on the extralinguistic context and can be regarded as an abstract manifestation of a conceptualising of real-world relations. Inner speech permits less reliance on concrete reality and enables flexible abstract thinking. Thus mental processing is not totally dependent on the external context. With higher intellectual functioning, there is increasingly a drawing on one's own internal mental resources rather than depending solely on the present external context. Both intralinguistic and extralinguistic knowledge are brought to bear on the regulation of activity.

Language development therefore proceeds from the social to the individual. Not only does the function of speech vary, but so too does its structure. As I have discussed in previous chapters, the form and content of language become more and more complex as children develop. While Vygotsky largely ignored aspects of the form of language, Wertsch (1980) attempted a semiotic analysis of language that extends and complements Vygotsky's analyses. In so doing, Wertsch examines in particular the social and individual functions of speech in relation to language as a mediational system. For example, speech on the interpsychological or social plane can consist of directives or commands to children by adults (Wertsch, 1985a, p. 92). In contrast, the intrapsychological or individual functions of speech are planning and regulatory. None the less, inner speech derives from social speech, as it is only through social interaction with another person that the functions of language that are culturally relevant and appropriate can be learned. Further social interaction facilitates word meaning in children since they construct meaning from understanding the speech of others. As Vygotsky claims (1986, p. 120), children do not spontaneously learn relations between objects and words. The meanings acquired are "predetermined by the meaning a given word already has in the language of adults".

Social Interaction, Practical Activity and Language

Although both speech and practical intelligence develop along separate lines during the early phases of a child's life, they do converge. The first manifestation of this convergence is when children are observed to talk while solving a complex problem. The example cited by Vygotsky (1978, p. 25)—from Levina—is that of a four-and-a-half year old child attempting to get candy from a cupboard with the assistance of a stool and a stick. In observing this activity, Levina noted that the girl chattered. This talk not only accompanied the action but also served to monitor and regulate it—it was both "natural and necessary".

According to Vygotsky, the experiments conducted by Levina demonstrated two important facts: one, that speech and action were united as one psychological function intended to accomplish the solution to a problem and, two, that the more complex the action and/or the more indirect the goal, the greater the role played by speech. Vygotsky (1978, p. 26) concludes that "... children solve practical tasks with the help of their speech, as well as their eyes and their hands".

Both egocentric language and social speech are involved in the solution of complex problems. Vygotsky further demonstrates the necessary link between these two forms of language. If children are required to solve an extremely difficult problem in the company of an adult—the mother or an experimenter perhaps—they may call for assistance (social speech) as well as regulating their actions by egocentric speech. If the adult does not respond to the child's pleas for help, the child will resort almost exclusively to egocentric language in an attempt to find a solution. The close interrelationship between the two forms of speech is however best characterised by the turning inwards of socialised speech. Speech requesting assistance, or interpersonal speech, becomes, with developmental time, intrapersonal speech, as children appeal to their own intellectual resources when solving a problem.

Social assistance is a necessary component to this developmental sequence. Adult assistance, or the potential for adult help, must be available for the child to use successfully the interpersonal functions of language needed to solve problems. Either when assistance is not available and/or with developmental time, such language functions become internalised. With the development of the intrapersonal functions of language comes the socialisation of practical mental activity. Speech in the early stages accompanies the action (as in Levina's example) but later comes to precede the action. Language becomes more insightful and takes on a planning function. Even later, language functions in more sophisticated ways and can determine and predict the course of the activity.

Fundamental to the whole process of the development of speech, the development of practical activity and the fusion of the two, is social interaction. In the course of solving a problem with another person, a child must communicate with that person. Both the cognitive and the communicative, the intrapersonal and the interpersonal functions of language are necessary for the development of human higher mental activity. Both aspects are inextricably linked and conjoined, and speech drives practical activity as well as practical activity driving the need for using language. In addition, both facilitate learning and result in cognitive development.

Learning in the Zone of Proximal Development

The central mechanism for learning (and in which instruction occurs) is the transfer of responsibility for the achievement of a mutually acceptable goal from the adult, the more expert or adept participant, to the child, the novice or naive participant, in collaborative interaction. The responsibility entails planning and monitoring the strategies for accomplishing success, operationalising the most expedient, efficient and efficacious strategies, assuming culpability for wrong decisions and demonstrating mastery of all aspects of the task. In so doing, success (i.e. attainment of the desired goal) is also usually achieved.

More formally, Vygotsky (1978, p. 86) postulated the existence of the "zone of proximal development", which is defined as the distance between the child's actual developmental level (as measured by conventional IQ tests for example), and her potential developmental level, as seen when a child is solving problems in interaction with "an adult or more capable peer". The zone of proximal development is thus a measure of learning potential. It represents the region wherein cognitive development takes place. It is important that the zone of proximal development be accorded a central position in the theory since it implies that the social environment, and the support and assistance it can offer, is crucial for development.

The zone of proximal development encompasses a number of notions as it is not simply a descriptive term for optimal learning and instruction. It implies a degree of collaboration between participants in the social interaction, where each is making a contribution towards the goal. These participants may come from different starting points and may not agree on the definition of the problem or the means to solve it. Part of the task of the zone of proximal development is to permit intersubjectivity and task definition (Wertsch, 1985c; Renshaw & Garton, 1984, 1986). Intersubjectivity occurs when the two participants share the same task, or situation definition, and each knows the other shares the same definition. Thus, not only is the child guided and supported to accomplishing the solution, he learns how to achieve mutuality and intersubjectivity, themselves instrumental to task success.

Part of the achievement of intersubjectivity relates to the contributions made by each participant in the interaction. Demarcation of roles facilitates learning, possibly for both participants. The novice or less competent participant determines the existing level of skill or expertise and sets the pace for instruction and learning. The more experienced participant gauges the pre-existing skills and the necessity for instruction and divides the task or problem into manageable components. The adult or more capable peer takes responsibility for the management of the task and also for changing the child's definition of the task. There is thus a dual role for the more experienced participant in the interaction, although these roles are indistinguishable in the instructional process.

As the zone of proximal development is a dynamic process, it is constantly changing. The adult's contribution must be altered in the face of the child's increasing competence and understanding. Instruction is always geared towards a higher level of functioning and Vygotsky (1956, cited in Wertsch, 1984) argued that "instruction creates a zone of proximal development". Social interaction provokes learning in the child and the zone of proximal development encapsulates the processes necessary for cognitive growth. Adult–child interaction and collaboration in an active and constantly changing situation allow for the development of culturally appropriate and relevant knowledge and skills in the child. The transmission of knowledge and technology pertinent to the prevailing socio-historical cultural context is of vast benefit to the developing child. It is in social interaction that such cognitive learning may occur.

It is useful to differentiate the zone of proximal development from the notion of scaffolding proposed by Bruner (1977) and discussed in Chapter 3. Scaffolding refers to the process of adult support and assistance given to a child mastering a locally determined problem. As noted previously, the problem might be a cognitive one or might be language *per se*, and the scaffolding can be horizontal or vertical. While this concept derives from Vygotsky's zone of proximal development, it has been extended along slightly different research lines. According to Wood (1988), scaffolding is the same as contingent teaching and refers to the sensitivity of a mother to a child's potential. The zone of proximal development is a theoretical construct that describes that potential, the distance between unaided and aided competence. Scaffolding refers to the aid component, with emphasis on the provision of appropriate support for successful learning. For Vygotsky, both the instructional component and the developmental component are integral, and his focus is on the child (or less competent) rather than on the instructional process *per se*.

McNaughton and Leyland (1990), in a study of maternal tutoring using problems of different difficulty levels, provide a useful distinction between scaffolding and the zone of proximal development. Scaffolding is considered as tutorial behaviour that is contingent, collaborative and interactive. It changes as a result of variations (usually increases) in the learner's abilities. McNaughton and Leyland point out that the research on scaffolding *assumes* the existence of a zone of proximal development by implying performance alone would be inferior. They further state that without an understanding of the existence of the zone of proximal development, the processes of scaffolding themselves cannot be fully understood. Underlying both concepts however is concern with the process of instruction and how individual competence is enhanced through the provision of social support and guidance. As Wertsch and Rogoff (1984) and Brown and Reeve (1987) point out, the notion of the facilitatory effect of social guidance has been applied to a range of research topics, mainly cognitive, and to the full age range from infancy to adolescence. All the contexts studied can broadly be grouped as problem solving, in so far as there is usually a desirable and achievable goal, which the more competent participant in the interaction has already accomplished or has the necessary knowledge or skills to solve. These are discussed in the next chapter.

SUMMARY

This chapter has examined the theories of Piaget and Vygotsky and their direct application in a range of research studies. In the case of Piaget's theory, the interactions studied contained conflict through opposing perspectives being presented by or to the participants. In most cases, these opposing perspectives were established by the differential capabilities demonstrated in pretesting. Conflict was the process whereby the interaction proceeded, and the entire point of the communicative interchange was the expression of the different views and their eventual resolution. Potentially all participants benefit from being exposed to different perspectives, but the cognitive gains are typically recorded in the initially less advanced participant.

Vygotsky's theory, on the other hand, assumes that social interaction involves the creation, establishment and maintenance of roles and task definitions for the mutual benefit of participants. Like many of the studies of socio-cognitive conflict, participants are of unequal cognitive status to begin with and are required to reach a consensus. Unlike the socio-cognitive studies, achievement of this end is via a process of instruction. A spirit of collaboration (in its broadest sense) is encouraged and facilitated by the use of language. This language fulfils a number of functions and captures the content of the interaction. Social interaction involves co-operation and assistance especially to the benefit of the learner.

CHAPTER FIVE

Conflict, Collaboration and Communication

All the research described so far in this book on social interaction and cognitive development has been derived from either Piaget's theory or Vygotsky's theory of development. The mechanisms postulated as accounting for cognitive growth in children have been social, dependent on interaction with another person—another child or an adult. In the studies conducted by Doise and his colleagues, a process of conflict within an interactive context is regarded as the mechanism responsible for cognitive change, whereas according to the research of Vygotsky, social assistance and language in the zone of proximal development are necessary facilitatory elements.

Derived from these two research strands are some recent studies that spawn both theories. In some cases, the studies have been directly inspired by one theoretical position but the results are best interpreted in the other framework, whereas in other instances a direct comparison was intended (e.g. Garton, 1983a). An increasing consensus over causal or facilitative mechanisms for cognitive growth is emerging from these studies, and in this chapter I wish to trace, by and large chronologically, this progression. It is useful to bear in mind that what emerges is that communication is essential for cognitive growth. For maximum advantage, this communication must be between active participants in collaborative social interaction and contain both conflict (as manifested in verbal and non-verbal disagreements) and agreement. Thus, the content of interactions can be characterised as being on a continuum

(Garton & Renshaw, 1988; Azmitia & Perlmutter, 1989) from conflict to agreement. The interactions might be productive or unproductive, might generate considerable communication and debate or none at all, and might achieve the intended solution. Profit in terms of cognitive gain from social interactions is dependent on the composition of the dyad (including age and sex), the nature of the task, and the levels of prior social and task-specific experience and knowledge the children bring to bear.

The studies to be described below all include an examination of the language used during social interaction in order to examine the facilitative role of communication. The Piagetian-inspired studies are described first, before a presentation of those studies inspired by Vygotsky's theory. However, demarcation between the studies becomes increasingly clouded, as methods and interpretations overlap. From these, I shall conclude with a unification of the important issues, prior to an examination of some important exceptions.

SOCIO-COGNITIVE CONFLICT AND LANGUAGE

Conflict Language

Some studies have specifically examined the actual language used during socio-cognitive conflict. Study of the communication between children during interaction sequences may reveal different types of language in relation to the success of the interaction, in terms of cognitive advancement. The language used during interactions may determine the nature and the extent of the learning that takes place. Or, the language may highlight the magnitude of the difference between alternative perspectives. In addition, analysis of the language may indicate how resolution of socio-cognitive conflict is achieved. This last issue has been investigated in some recent research, each study having slightly different aims, using different analyses and, yet all conclude by questioning the Piagetian conflict model as being the best explanation for how social interaction advances cognition in children.

Bearison, Magzamen and Filardo (1986) purported to compare group and individual performances of children on a spatial perspective task as well as teasing out the critical aspects of the interaction that might be benefiting certain subjects. Interestingly, they did not find marked improvements from pretest to posttest scores in children who had engaged in social interaction. However, they do report a curvilinear relationship only in boys between verbal explanations in conflicts and cognitive change scores. That is, there was an optimal number of task-related disagreements which when resolved with appropriate explanation would benefit the dyadic partners. Too many or too few were counter-productive.

The discovery of a curvilinear relationship between verbal conflict and cognitive change was a new finding and Bearison et al. discuss the nature of these verbal disagreements. Only those with explanations attached were found to be beneficial. Dyads were designated as balanced or unbalanced in terms of the number of conflicts expressed by the respective partners. Dyadic partners who disagreed with each other in a relatively balanced pattern had significantly greater cognitive gains. An unbalanced generation of the conflict did not enhance cognitive growth. Thus, there is a fairly limited number and type of disagreements per interaction sequence that optimises subsequent cognitive development, and these are only recorded in boys. It is speculated that this sex difference illustrates a difference in the way boys and girls are socialised to interact with one another. Bearison et al. (1986) conclude that, to be of cognitive benefit, socio-cognitive conflicts should occur in a cooperative social context. To this should be added the fact the socio-cognitive conflict is manifested in verbal disagreements, and only a limited range of these is linked to cognitive development. The finding is consistent with the model proposed by Doise since the verbal expression of different (and perhaps opposing) task strategies allows children to co-ordinate their different perspectives or solutions and facilitates the achievement of a single satisfactory result.

Garton and Renshaw (1988) also examined the disagreements that occurred during peer interaction. The focus of this research was not on the relationship between the nature and type of disagreements and success (or otherwise) on the cognitive tasks, but instead was on the language used in the disagreements. Pairs of children were classified on the basis of the extent of their collaboration in the early stages of the interaction. This was achieved by how quickly they established specific and differentiated roles, how much interactive language they used to communicate with one another, and how successfully they completed the task. A continuum of collaboration emerged, ranging from pairs who spoke little, showed no role differentiation and often did not complete the task, to communicative, differentiated pairs who usually completed the task—though not always to the experimenter's specifications (Garton, 1992). These pairs were then predictive of the form of the disagreement and its resolution. Disagreements were characterised by non-verbal or verbal (or both) dispute over the appropriate next block or the placement of a block. Resolution of the dispute required negotiation (and counter-negotiation) and sometimes capitulation of one child. The disagreement was the focal point of the conversational exchange, often marked by the word "No".

An examination of all the instances of disagreement indicated that while no sex differences were recorded, there was a developmental trend in the events that triggered disagreements and the linguistic means used to resolve such arguments. Older children had verbal as opposed to non-verbal disputes and further progress depended on mutual satisfaction as to the resolution of the disagreement. Again, Bearison et al. (1986) and Garton and Renshaw (1988) believe that an analysis of the language used during peer interaction can provide clues for the mechanisms necessary for the achievement of a single, unified solution to a problem. Overt verbal conflict does arise when children are attempting to reach a satisfactory response and the expression of this (both its form and content) may highlight at least some of the processes involved in social interaction.

Azmitia (1988) also sought to examine, among other things, what features of the social interaction between "novice" and "expert" children promoted learning. This she did by comparing the relation between their disagreements and learning. "Novices" and "experts" were determined on the basis of pretest scores and assigned to experimental groups of same ability or mixed ability or to work alone. A spatial copying task was used in the interaction sequence. Measurement of the mechanisms of facilitation included conflict, which was defined as a sequence of three verbal disagreements. However conflict did not mediate success in the interaction task. Further, of the other postulated mediators (viz. observational learning and guidance by an expert), expert guidance, which ought to contribute to improved performance in novices, was not evidenced. Experts spent little time monitoring the performance of their novice partners. Observation only increased with time and it was difficult to gauge its contribution to learning. No comparison was made between the groups, although it appears that mixed-ability groups had more conflict sequences than same-ability groups. Azmitia explains the lack of a mediating effect for conflict in terms of the failure of the preschoolers in her study to sustain discourse over a period of time, and perhaps her specification of three disagreements as constituting conflict is too stringent.

Interestingly, these three studies all make reference to Vygotsky and his theory of learning. Bearison et al. (1986), Garton and Renshaw (1988) and Azmitia (1988) all believe Vygotsky's collaborative theory of learning offers an explanation that accounts for cognitive development. Bringing the language of the interaction sequence into consideration forces the inclusion of alternative theoretical positions. Certainly Garton and Renshaw, and Azmitia find Vygotsky's theory has greater explanatory power than Piaget's conflict theory in relation to the effects of language in social interaction. Instead of invoking socio-cognitive conflict *per se* (and as evidenced via conflict language), collaboration including mutual communication, disagreement and negotiation, may maximise cognitive growth. Integration of these studies with those conducted under a Vygotskian rubric will be attempted later in this chapter.

Communication and Conflict

Explicit comparisons between socio-cognitive conflict and communication as mechanisms for cognitive development are rare. Even more rare are experimental attempts to confirm one or the other, to demonstrate the superiority of either one over the other, or to investigate the relationship between communication and cognitive development. Azmitia's (1988) study represents an attempt to do this. Garton (1983a, 1986) described the background to a study designed to achieve this. Experimental pairings of same-ability (collaborative) and mixed-ability (conflict) children were constructed and then a longitudinal study of their interaction sequences when solving problems undertaken. The communication of the pairs was investigated, as was the success of the interaction and generalisation and maintenance in posttests. As reported in Garton and Renshaw (1988), the final pairs studied could not be described as either conflict or collaborative, and a collaboration continuum was preferred to describe the interaction process. Other variables such as age were more important predictors of the types of conflict sequences recorded and their utility in advancing progress on the task. Pretest ability was not predictive of the extent or magnitude of conflict in the interaction sequences. Hence, an examination of the communication processes as they related to conflict (as the content of the interaction measured by verbal disagreements) was undertaken as described above.

Luque Lozano (1988), adopting a socio-cognitive orientation, analysed the language during several social interaction conditions where children were required to work together to solve a problem. Like Garton, he found inconsistencies in his results with social interaction not always being sufficient for cognitive development. Verbal interaction skills, as measured by the use of discourse features like anaphora and deixis, were a better predictor of cognitive change than social interaction *per se*. He believed that a context permitting the expression of shared reference was the most beneficial for cognitive development. Again, Vygotsky's theory, with its emphasis on the social bases for the development of knowledge, was invoked as the preferred, and more suitable, explanation.

Phelps and Damon (1987) discuss productive strategies in social interaction that provoke cognitive growth. Both socio-cognitive conflict and collaboration are included amongst these strategies and are explicitly compared in their study. The analyses examine macro-level changes and focus on transcribed communicative sequences. For my purposes here, I will confine my discussion to those aspects of the language related to previous studies presented. Neither agreeing with nor disagreeing with one's partner was predictive of cognitive change. Rather, partners who both agreed *and* disagreed showed most change. Phelps and Damon believe this is indicative of a style of communication characterised by a responsiveness to the other partner. This includes being agreeable and being disagreeable. Further, those who developed cognitively were also likely to be asked for clarification by the other partner.

Like Garton and Renshaw (1988), Phelps and Damon find that communication "style" is important for cognitive development. Learning was most noticeable in children who were communicatively responsive, who listened and responded to the other participant and who clarified their own statements when required. Phelps and Damon conclude that a collaborative explanation for cognitive growth accords best with their results, rather than a socio-cognitive conflict explanation. They believe that the verbal construction of a collaborative relationship between the children in the interaction can produce a mutually acceptable solution to the problem as well as promoting cognitive development.

Socio-cognitive conflict therefore has been studied in a number of ways. Many of the studies have shown that such conflict, presented either socially, cognitively or verbally, is an important component in cognitive advancement. Conflict however should be regarded as the content of the interaction rather than as a process in its own right. Thus, during social interaction the presentation of a point of view different to one's own forces a child to reconsider her own perspective. In so doing, the child may accept the new point of view or reject the new position, but whatever the outcome, she will have given measured consideration to the different answers. When a single solution to a task problem is required, children will be forced to evaluate and (re)consider a number of perspectives. The adoption of a cognitively more advanced position is evidence of cognitive gain. There is no doubt that such gains do accrue after social interaction, and specifically after socially induced cognitive conflict. Not all the researchers endorse Piaget's original theoretical writings because, as will be demonstrated in the next section, there are other theoretical explanations that can account for the cognitive benefits of social interaction.

JOINT PROBLEM SOLVING

A joint problem-solving context is the ideal situation in which to examine the process of social interaction between an adult and a child, or between participants with different degrees of competence. Typically such contexts are instructional and provide for the creation of a zone of proximal development (cf. Wertsch, 1984). The processes whereby intersubjectivity is achieved and the responsibility for solving the problem or attaining the task goal can be studied in either an experimental or a naturalistic context. Setting a problem to solve allows the experimenter to study all the aspects of the zone of proximal development.

Vygotsky's theory has given rise to a number of studies which have examined in detail the processes of social interaction between young children and adults, usually their mothers, or more capable peers. I will now consider some illustrative research studies. Some of the studies to be discussed have examined how cognitively mature parents (and sometimes other adults) guide and monitor the problem-solving behaviour of their children (e.g. Wertsch, McNamee, McLane & Budwig, 1980; Rogoff & Gardner, 1984). Other studies have examined peer interaction and its facilitative effect on children's levels of cognitive competence (for reviews see Gauvain & Rogoff, 1989, and Tudge & Rogoff, 1989). Both adult–child and child–child interaction during problem solving will be examined below.

Adult–child Interaction

A popular problem-solving task, and one used extensively by Wertsch and his colleagues (Wertsch et al., 1980), involves a mother–child dyad working together to create an object in accordance with a provided model, rather like a jigsaw puzzle (see Fig. 5.1). In such a situation, there is transfer of responsibility from the mother to the child for the completion of the task. Task, or jigsaw, completion includes various definable aspects—such as checking the picture on the box, locating the correct piece and inserting it in the jigsaw—which ensure regulation and monitoring of the task. Initially, these are the mother's responsibility but once the child realises their strategic significance, he adopts them and monitors his own problem-solving behaviours. Not only is there an instructional component, there is the negotiation of a mutually acceptable definition of the task. The two participants approach the task differently and, in the process of achieving the goal demanded by the experimenter, also negotiate intersubjectivity, that is, a common shared definition of the task and its goals. As Wertsch (1984)

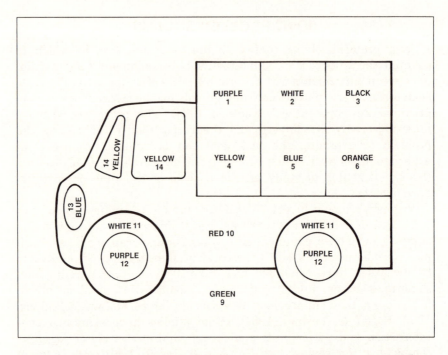

FIG. 5.1 Jigsaw puzzle used in joint problem-solving task (Wertsch et al., 1980)

points out, negotiating the mutually acceptable definition of the task
(that subsequently defines the zone of proximal development) often
requires the child to alter her understanding of objects and events. It
may not mean that the child adapts to the adult's position as sometimes
a compromise is necessary for the task to proceed. The adopted
intersubjective view of the task may thus require both participants to
shift from their original intrapsychological perspective. None the less,
the position communicated by the adult is generally a transient,
task-specific perspective, adopted to facilitate the child's understanding
of the task to permit task completion. The change in the child's position,
to a qualitatively different interpretation of the task, hence to a higher
level of understanding or representation, is a more permanent shift and
is the product of the instructional process.

The particular behaviours selected by Wertsch et al. (1980) for
studying the process of jigsaw completion included both verbal and
non-verbal behaviours used by the mother to regulate the child. These
were examined in particular in relation to the square "cargo" jigsaw
pieces differentiated only by colour and not shape (see Fig. 5.1). The
child's gaze to the model was taken as the measure of success of the

mother's strategy. The study involved mother–child pairs, the children being aged two-and-a-half, three-and-a-half or four-and-a-half years. All verbal utterances were transcribed from video recordings made of the interactions, as were the pointing gestures and the handling of the jigsaw puzzle pieces by both the mother and the child. Transfer of responsibility for regulating task completion was measured by the child's consultation of the model as witnessed by the number of eye gazes and when in the sequence they occurred.

The actual number of gazes varied between dyads and the mean number fluctuated, resulting in no significant age-related differences. What was of greater interest was the regulation of these gazes—whether they were mother(other)-regulated or child(self)-regulated. Mother-regulated gazes occurred if the mother pointed to the model, made explicit verbal reference to the necessary puzzle piece or made implicit reference for the need to consult the model. If the mother did not exhibit any of these behaviours, the gaze was coded as self-regulated. Basically what Wertsch et al. found was that other-regulated gazes decreased significantly with age. This means that, with increasing age, there is less dependence on regulation of the task by another person. In addition, further analyses revealed that when younger children did consult the model themselves, they were unable to capitalise on this action. They either failed to use the information to make a correct decision about which puzzle piece to insert or could not infer the relevant information from the model. Either way, according to Wertsch et al., they did not realise the strategic significance of consulting the model.

As there were age differences in the extent to which children took responsibility for completing the jigsaw puzzle, Wertsch et al. (1980) then examined their data for evidence of "microgenetic" progress. They found that, whereas within an interaction session individual dyads might show progress, overall there was no evidence to support microgenetic change. Ontogenetic change from other- to self-regulation in relation to consultation of the model was marked and taken as evidence of a shift from interpsychological to intrapsychological functioning.

Child–child Interaction

Peer interaction characterised the research discussed in the previous chapter by the Genevan group led by Doise. It was concluded from these studies and other similar experiments that it was difficult to specify exactly the nature of the interaction that facilitated cognitive growth. It was further concluded that verbal expression of opposing perspectives was one important contributory factor, and one that provoked cognitive growth through a process of evaluation and reconsideration of one's own perspective. I suggested in Chapter 4 that collaboration might represent better than conflict the nature of such interactions and that a Vygotskian perspective might offer greater explanatory power than a post-Piagetian one.

Forman and Cazden (1985) distinguish between different forms of peer interaction with reference to a teaching context. Peer tutoring, involving reciprocal teaching between children, is compared to peer collaboration as investigated by Doise and his colleagues (e.g. Doise & Mugny, 1984). They believe that the latter research where peer interaction involves the integration of a variety of different perspectives to promote cognitive development is important particularly in relation to classroom teaching practices. Forman and Cazden then describe a study of peer collaboration in which they examine the processes of the social interactional sequences rather than focusing on the outcome performance measures of cognitive growth. In so doing, they intend to isolate those social processes most responsible for cognitive growth.

Drawing on both Vygotskian-inspired research and the Piagetian tradition, Forman and Cazden's study involved the videotaping of collaborative problem-solving sessions. A modified variant of the type of design used by Perret-Clermont (1980) was adopted for a longitudinal study. Both social interactional patterns and problem-solving strategies were examined across 11 sessions in four pairs of children of approximately nine years of age. A control group of single children also participated in the longitudinal study. A chemical combination task (after Piaget) was used in all sessions, with different chemical reactions being demonstrated which the children were required to reproduce.

Forman and Cazden analysed only the part of the sessions devoted to the planning and setting up of the experiments necessary to show the demonstrated chemical colour change. Only data from three subject pairs across four sessions are reported by Forman and Cazden with a narrow focus on only one form of social behaviour—namely, procedural interactions, plus three problem-solving strategies. Procedural interactions were coded as parallel, associative or cooperative (after Parten, 1932), the three representing increasing co-ordination of roles and sharing of ideas. The three problem-solving strategies of random/trial-and-error, isolation of the variables and combinatorial represent increasingly sophisticated approaches to experimentation.

On pretest to posttest measures on an unrelated task, the children who had worked in pairs were no different to the children who had worked alone. On posttesting on the chemical combination problem task, the paired children performed marginally better. However, during the sessions where the chemical combination problems had to be solved, the pairs were more efficient, working at a faster rate. The successful and speedy strategies adopted by children working in pairs were not translated consistently to individual performance, especially on an unfamiliar task. Forman and Cazden explain this lack of success of collaboration in terms of the small number of dyads involved in the study. Big differences between dyads may mask differences between children from pairs and singletons.

Examination of the procedural interactions showed that the dyads predominantly engaged in parallel or associative patterns during the first interaction session. The extent of cooperation varied from dyad to dyad, and one pair did not cooperate at all across the 11 sessions. The pair who rapidly used a cooperative experimental strategy solved the greatest number of chemical problems overall, although the high levels of performance were not noted in the posttest measures.

As cognitive conflict was not measured, it is difficult to make a direct comparison of this study with that of Perret-Clermont (1980) even though conflicting perspectives were recorded. However conflicting processes were neither generated spontaneously nor by design. Dyads were formed to maximise collaboration and during the early phases of the problem-solving session analysed, overt conflict or disagreement was rare. The experimentation strategies elicited during the setting-up phase revealed differing levels of cooperation and division of roles. Those pairs adopting a close cooperative pattern offered mutual support, guidance, encouragement and an equitable, often complementary, division of duties. The distinction between the setting-up phase and the actual (unanalysed) experimental stage may be based on two different interactive processes—a collaborative pattern and, later, a less collaborative one, characterised by the expression of argument or disagreement.

Although Forman and Cazden attempt to reconcile their results with those of Perret-Clermont, they find Vygotsky's theory more accommodating to their findings. In interactions where there is no overt conflict, but instead mutual cooperation, Vygotsky's theory is able to explain the greater success of the dyads when working on the problems together. Interpersonal regulation of task behaviour may occur in such dyads since neither partner has objectively more competence than the other. By adopting complementary roles, they can maximise the interaction since one child can observe, guide and monitor the task and the other can actually undertake the task procedures. It is claimed that the adoption of complementary social roles benefits *both* children cognitively, since both are working in a zone of proximal development created by the very nature of the problem. Interpersonal regulation can quickly become intrapersonal regulation, witnessed in eventual cognitive growth. Forman and Cazden discuss in depth the utility of Vygotsky's theory in collaborative contexts where there is no conflict.

In order to reconcile the two theoretical explanations, it is necessary to consider the notion of the shared task perspective. Conflicting perspectives, communicated by children during collaborative problem solving, may indeed prompt cognitive development (as might agreement between strategies: Bryant, 1982; Chambers, 1990). Reconciling different points of view generated by children who have different perspectives on the task and the social interaction may be one way in which children can advance cognitively. Children can integrate opposing positions, evaluate different positions and modify existing cognitions. Alternatively, and more importantly, social regulation of activities may equally benefit children cognitively, because the assuming of complementary roles within an interaction also permits communication. Such social regulation via communication about role division, task planning and execution can permit the solving of more difficult problems by pairs than by children working alone. Mutual benefits accrue to children who can work together, communicate, and debate successfully and achieve mastery of the task. In both instances, however, communication between participants is the key to success, in terms of satisfactory completion of the task and possibly in terms of more general cognitive development.

Finding the Appropriate Level of Collaborative Functioning

These studies of adult–child and child–child problem solving have illustrated how social interaction can facilitate both negotiation of intersubjectivity (or the meeting of minds) and successful completion of the problem or task. Behaviours relevant to the process have been identified and analysed for their contribution to the child's cognitive development. The fundamental role played by communication between participants has again been highlighted. The use of the zone of proximal development, created via the instructional component and enabling cognitive growth has thus been well documented.

However, it is only at the macro level that commonalities between the various studies can be found. At the micro level, it is clear that it is difficult to prescribe the optimal level of collaboration that will facilitate cognitive development. Azmitia and Perlmutter (1989) suggest that important variables to include, at least in studies of peer interaction, are the ages of the children, their sexes, the level of task difficulty, the children's level(s) of expertise and task familiarity. Systematic study of all these variables concomitantly has not yet been undertaken and

Azmitia and Perlmutter suggest that a first study should examine the role of age and task difficulty in social interactive contexts. A goal of future research should be to establish the relationship between task difficulty/familiarity and the magnitude and effects of collaborative problem solving.

Freund (1990) describes a study in which she compares maternal regulation of a child's behaviour in a problem-solving task with a situation where the child receives only corrective feedback. Freund's study is particularly impressive because of the comprehensiveness of her design and because it permits a comparative assessment of different aspects of a problem-solving task previously examined independently. Her aims are no different to those of other investigators, namely the study of the relative effectiveness of mother–child interaction on subsequent child performance, but she adds an examination of the division of task responsibility as a function of child age, task difficulty and task or strategic component. She included these additional variables in her study because, as she argues, investigators tend to use only age as a measure of initial (in)competence without varying other dimensions of task performance. Age is also often the only independent variable in the task. She further claims that many of the social interaction studies have failed to find convincing generalisation effects possibly due to not taking into account some of these other variables.

In order to establish what might be ideal conditions for the achievement of self-regulation in a child, she therefore varied task difficulty (easy vs. difficult), child age (three- vs. five-year-old) and what she termed task component, namely strategically relevant important behaviours. The important variables in the study were those related to maternal responsibility, or task components. In the sorting task, three components were identified—item selection, room selection and item placement—and three levels of control and regulation of these—mother responsible, mother regulation and child self-regulation. That is, the mother could actually perform the sorting task or a component of it, regulate the child's activities, or the child could regulate her own behaviour and take responsibility for one or more of the components.

Individual levels of ability on a furniture sorting task were assessed first. The task required the sorting of a varying number of pieces of model furniture (and distractor items) and positioning them together appropriately in a room in a doll's house. Children were not told the names of the rooms, nor was any particular floorplan expected of them. Children then either worked alone, supported by corrective feedback for errors given by the experimenter, or worked in interaction with their mothers. The mothers were instructed to help their children, not to teach them. Easy and difficult versions of the task for each age group were used (after extensive pilot testing) involving varying the number of rooms and the number of pieces of furniture and their potential groupings; one of the outcome measures was accuracy of sorting the materials. In broad terms, there was an improvement in performance with age across both conditions, feedback and interaction, with the five-year-old children showing improved individual performance after both conditions.

Freund (1990) claims her study shows that social interaction facilitates improved independent task performance as accuracy of sorting was enhanced to a greater extent in posttesting by children who had participated in the interaction condition. They also showed greater gains. The analyses conducted on the data are thorough and quite complex, and extrapolation here is based solely on crucial but interesting results. There were no effects associated with order of task difficulty presentation, but for both age groups mothers were more likely to regulate the crucial task component (selection of a room appropriate for the furniture) in the difficult version of the task. With the younger children, mothers were more likely to regulate that task component than the selection of an item, in this case a piece of furniture. Responsibility also varied with task difficulty, with mothers tending to assume total responsibility in the difficult task, particularly for room selection. Overall however, responsibility was taken by mothers for item selection.

Maternal language was also analysed and although there were differences in the amount of language produced per dyad, mothers of the younger children tended to offer more specific, concrete advice and guidance and, with the more difficult version of the task, made reference to particular task strategies. In her discussion, Freund focuses on the beneficial effects of social interaction on subsequent child performance and relates this improvement to specific aspects of the interaction. The task or strategy components studied and the extent of the regulation by the mother and her child indicated that mothers were sensitive to the demands of the task, especially the difficult version. They also varied the extent of their regulation as a function of the child's age. Dividing the task into components permitted detailed analysis of relevant aspects of the interaction that were facilitating regulation of the task by the child. It is evident that analysing task and strategic components in social problem solving validates Vygotsky's theory and the zone of proximal development in particular. Assuming responsibility through a process of other- to self-regulation enables the child to monitor her own behaviours together with an increased understanding of the task and the mechanisms of interaction. Self-directed problem solving leads not only to improved task success, but also, it is claimed by Kontos and Nicholas (1986), to increased cognitive skill.

Azmitia and Perlmutter (1989) provide a very useful review of research on social interaction and cognitive development. They compare and contrast a number of theoretical models, concluding with a comparison between the two leading perspectives, namely those of Piaget and Vygotsky. In discussing the impact of social agents on cognitive changes, Azmitia and Perlmutter discuss a number of influences such as members of the family and opportunities for peer interaction in the preschool years. Their discussion of peer interaction is of particular interest, because, as noted previously, they make an attempt to identify the relevant variables that ought to be included in studies of peer collaboration. Further, they extend their review to examine the relationship between learning and friendship and learning and interaction style. Finally, they offer a framework for considering developmental change in social influences in cognition. Rather than regarding the impact of social influences as unidimensional, they argue for a consideration of changing levels of facilitatory mechanisms. This model will be described at length in Chapter 6, but suffice it to say at this stage that it goes a long way towards accommodating the results of a diverse range of research studies and to providing valid *developmental* explanations of the influence of social interaction.

Social Interaction, Self-regulation and Metacognition

In social interaction, especially between an adult and a child, it has been claimed that there is a shift of the responsibility for monitoring and control from the adult to the child. Responsibility for strategic control is evidenced in self-regulation, itself manifested in self-correction and self-directed learning.

Such notions of monitoring and control are compatible with the central concepts of metacognition. According to Flavell (1978), metacognition involves both knowledge and cognition about cognitive phenomena including memory, language and problem solving. The essential components of metacognition are an ability to understand and to think about one's cognitive experiences and to be aware of under what circumstances (social events, tasks and people) to invoke and deploy them. In addition to metacognition referring to knowledge of one's own cognitive processes, it has also been used in the literature to refer to regulation of these processes (Brown, 1978). In some cases there has been confusion about exactly which meaning is intended (for a discussion see Freund, 1990; Bialystok, 1992). Cognitive self-regulation is only partially synonymous with metacognition as the emphasis is much more on the regulatory aspect rather than the knowledge aspect.

Freund (1990) equates the regulatory component of metacognition with cognitive self-regulation. Cognitive self-regulation is then discussed in relation both to Vygotsky's theory and to studies of children's problem-solving activities (e.g. Wertsch, Minick & Arns, 1984) and to adult regulation of children's learning (e.g. Wertsch et al., 1980). The shift from other-regulation to self-regulation occurs with a shift of responsibility for control in problem-solving contexts.

Brown and Reeve (1987) discuss both social interaction and self-regulation as possible mechanisms that encourage cognitive growth, citing illustrative research for both positions. Brown and Reeve mention overtly social contexts (with adult or peer assistance) or covertly social contexts in which thinking is modified in response to an internalised "audience". They coin the phrase "bandwidths of competence" to refer to the fact that different (social vs. internal) interactions may be appropriate for differently created zones of proximal development. In their review, they provide research support for both overt and covert social processes operating in differently created zones of proximal development, the former being illustrated by studies such as those inspired by Vygotsky's theory and the latter by the work of Flavell (1978) and that of Brown (1978) herself on aspects of metacognitive and self-regulatory development.

Learning and development are argued to be interdependent, a Vygotskian theoretical construct. Naturally occurring contexts create opportunities for both learning and development, with support, either socially overt or covert, being necessary. Interactional contexts, broadly defined, provide for cognitive development and indeed drive cognitive growth. While the instructional component is not clearly specified, Brown and Reeve draw attention to the contexts that can permit both development and learning in young children, contexts that provide adequate and appropriate support.

Language and Communication in the Zone of Proximal Development

Language is one medium used to transmit regulatory behaviours. More generally, the social transmission by language of culture and cultural conventions—including the conventional and acceptable uses of language—is essential for cognitive development. Bruner (1984) makes this point forcefully when he discusses the "hidden agenda" of the zone of proximal development. Underlining Vygotskian adherence to Marxism and the collective consciousness, he draws parallels between the development of a child and the modernisation of the peasant. In both cases, according to Bruner (1984, p. 94), socio-historical cultural knowledge is transmitted by the meeting of the minds (or "mental sharing". Language is the medium that allows such transmission. It is consistent with Marxist theory, Bruner argues, because language (broadly conceived to include natural language and the language of science and maths) is an historically conditioned instrument. Language permits the sharing of collective consciousness and the transgenerational expression of both new and old knowledge. In addition, Vygotsky (see the study discussed by Luria, 1976) was acutely aware of the impact of literacy on increasing the collective consciousness and skills of the peasants. Why, Bruner argues, should it not be the same for the developing child?

Analyses of the language used by collaborators in the zone of proximal development have revealed inconsistent results. Interactions where verbal disagreements are recorded (Bearison et al., 1986; Azmitia, 1988; Garton & Renshaw, 1988) seem to indicate that overt expression of areas where different perspectives prevail is useful, though the level and nature of these disagreements is unclear. This contention is further supported by the work and speculations of Forman and Cazden (1985), who hypothesise that analysing problem-solving contexts by examining sub-goals may shed further light on the most facilitative type of interaction and communication for cognitive growth. To a certain extent, the study by Freund (1990) achieves this aim. Her analysis of the verbal content of mothers' language during the furniture sorting task revealed more maternal verbalisations during the more difficult task. The actual content of the verbalisations also varied, with, for example, mothers of the three-year-old children making more references to task strategies during the difficult task, and mothers of five-year-old children making more reference to plans, goals and monitoring. None the less, Freund's discussion pays little attention to the verbal aspects of the tasks since they did not relate to the division of the task into the components that were used in her regulatory analysis. In fact, such an analysis would be difficult to undertake because of the range and diversity of the language used by mothers during the study.

It can be quite validly concluded that language undoubtedly plays a crucial role in the collaborative efforts of problem solvers. Whether the content *per se* matters or whether more global categories of language function are sufficient to capture those essential aspects awaits closer scrutiny. Unfortunately, experimentally this is the most difficult variable to control, mainly because of large individual differences in maternal speech style (both quantity and quality). The same is true for peer interaction and both Forman and Cazden (1985) and Garton and Renshaw (1988) report large between-dyad differences in the extent of the communication between the children. This issue will be discussed at greater length and depth in the next chapter, where a synthesis of the range of topics discussed so far will be undertaken.

SOCIAL INTERACTION AND COGNITIVE DEVELOPMENT IN HEARING-IMPAIRED CHILDREN

It has been contended throughout this chapter that collaborative communication, conceived of as language used in interaction, is an, if not the, important mediator in social interaction for cognitive development. What happens when conventional verbal language is not available, as in the case of severely hearing-impaired children? Many of these children have alternative means of communicating, and some research studies have been conducted to see if the hearing deficit *per se* impairs performance on both socio-cognitive conflict tasks and tutoring tasks. This permits an examination of whether it is language or conversational communication that is supportive of the cognitive gains recorded in experimental tasks.

Socio-cognitive Conflict and Deafness

Peterson and Peterson (1991) examine the socio-cognitive skills of young hearing-impaired children in a spatial perspective-taking task, and whether being given the opportunity to discuss the tasks and its solution(s) with other children does indeed lead to cognitive gain. Deaf children typically lag cognitively behind their hearing peers and Peterson and Peterson conjecture whether this delay is the result of a failure (or lack of opportunity) to consider or to be exposed to alternatives during development. Deaf children often have limited social experience, in terms of normal interactions with others. Such social interactions that do take place are often restricted both spatially and temporally, for a range of reasons. It has also been claimed that deaf children are socialised into more passive roles, rarely challenging or being challenged by others. This may impede cognitive development. According to the stronger theory of impairment, deaf children will not benefit from social conflict since they are unable to deal with confrontation and challenge. However, if deaf children simply have less experience with social interactions, then cognitive conflict should produce cognitive gains, as with the hearing children in the experiments discussed previously.

All the children involved in the study used signing as their means of communication, and all were rated as proficient signers. Peterson and Peterson (1991) found that after socio-cognitive conflict on a spatial perspective-taking task (from Doise & Mugny, 1984), deaf children did show enhanced cognitive performance on posttests. Using a range of error scores, those children who had participated in social interaction showed significant decreases in errors compared to a control group who had no such social experience. It was concluded that "peer debate" facilitated cognitive development in these deaf children in much the same way as has been recorded for hearing children. The means by which conflict appeared to be facilitative were also similar in that the deaf children saw contradictions in the solutions proposed by the other child and disagreed actively (by signing and by repositioning items). However, while a study such as this casts doubt on the centrality of conventional spoken language as a mediating mechanism in cognitive development, it supports the view that active involvement in the task and the opportunity to contradict or disagree in a communicative context with the other partner are powerful aspects of the social interaction that facilitate cognitive development.

Tutoring and Deafness

Instead of considering cognitive conflict, which he judges to be inadequate to capture processes of learning, Wood (1989) adopts a perspective that emphasises learning arising from the interaction of a more knowledgeable individual and a less knowledgeable one. This position owes much to Vygotsky, and Wood has extended it to incorporate the learning processes of hearing-impaired children. According to Wood (1989), a hearing impairment (or deafness) is likely to impact on a child's development because of secondary handicapping conditions that arise as a result of the sensory disability. Wood (1989, p. 62) believes that these secondary handicaps are a "consequence of the impact of the child's disability on processes of social interaction that normally serve implicit tutoring functions and that facilitate the transmission of culture and competence". In other words, the hearing impairment disrupts the normal formation of social relationships and this in turn has an impact on the teaching–learning process. Deaf children characteristically show delays in language and cognitive development. These, Wood argues, are ramifications of the disrupted social interactions that occur (consciously or inadvertently) as a result of the child's hearing impairment. This position is stated quite forcefully by Wood (1989, p. 67): "the transmission of knowledge and the facilitation of understanding are threatened not simply by impeded access to sound, but by distorted and sometimes destructive effects of deafness on processes of natural tutoring and more formal teaching".

In his extensive research with deaf children, Wood (1980), together with his colleagues, has investigated, amongst other things, the disrupted processes of learning and instruction. By examining the interactions of deaf children and their tutors (who were teachers of the deaf) during a problem-solving task, Wood found that children who were assigned tutors who were sensitive and responded contingently were more competent and successful when completing the task alone afterwards. As is the case with hearing children (Wood, 1988), deaf children show greatest gains on problem-solving tasks when instructed in a measured and empathic manner. The cognitive delays demonstrated by hearing-impaired children are likely to be a result of inadequate and perhaps distorted social interaction which is mirrored in inappropriate instructional processes. A desire to help the deaf child communicate and learn produces "over-scaffolding", inhibiting the natural language and cognitive development of the child (Wood, 1989).

The preceding research studies have shown that deaf children can clearly benefit from social interaction, either via cognitive conflict or by participation in a tutorial or instructional process. The communication mechanism utilised in interactions of hearing children and adults may be impaired resulting in language and/or cognitive delay, but the *processes* by which gains can be achieved seem remarkably similar. Peterson and Peterson (1991) argue for the efficacy of socio-cognitive conflict, while Wood prefers an account that emphasises a tutorial process that takes account of the needs of the child. The arguments are identical to those discussed previously in relation to the hearing child and permit a greater understanding on our part of some of the mechanisms responsible for cognitive change.

SUMMARY

In summarising the research in this chapter, together with that described in the previous chapter, it is useful to synthesise the issues into important hypotheses. The key theoretical concept that derives from the Genevan-inspired research on social interaction is *conflict*—or *socio-cognitive conflict* to be specific. The occurrence of conflict as an interactive process implies negotiation and resolution, both apparently efficacious indicators of cognitive growth. The superiority of pairs of children over the solitary individual in facilitating cognitive growth emerges as an important aspect of the research.

Social interaction encourages debate and conflict, the basis of which is a partnership between participants, reliant for its establishment and maintenance on *communication*. To communicate successfully means the negotiation of common ground to achieve the goal of the task. A *shared task perspective* (in whatever domain) facilitates the accomplishment of the task plus it encourages cognitive growth by the presentation and discussion of alternatives. Thus the theoretical mechanisms apparently underpinning cognitive growth are derivative from social interaction which encourages communication in general, and conflict, negotiation and resolution in particular.

From Vygotskian-inspired research comes the concept of *collaboration* as a way of describing the process of interaction and communication, *instruction* and *learning*. This perspective accords well with the key concepts identified above and can be synthesised into a vision of social interaction being facilitative for cognitive development because of the opportunity it provides for discussion. Communication (at whatever level, be it verbal or non-verbal) characterises a collaborative continuum. Within this continuum, it can be postulated that conflict is one extreme. Conflict may thus contrast with collaboration at the other extreme or be regarded as a form of collaboration characterised by disagreement and argument, rather than agreement and cooperation. Conflict, operationalised as disagreement, may be efficacious for cognitive growth. The more communication and the more negotiation and resolution that takes place over differences in opinion regarding role delineation or task strategy, the more collaborative are the dyads—and, as a corollary, the more collaborative the dyads, the greater the level of success on the task and the greater the cognitive gains and benefits. Aspects of this model still require testing, but it represents a respectable attempt at a reconciliation of two different perspectives. Synthesising these key concepts with the theoretical constructs derived from the language development research is the challenge in Chapter 6.

CHAPTER SIX

Social Mechanisms of Development

The previous four chapters have highlighted different strands of developmental research that have demonstrated the usefulness and effectiveness of considering social interaction as an important factor in development. The developmental strength of social interaction ranges from direct and causal to more indirect, perhaps mediational. I wish now here to draw together the main conclusions from each of the areas covered (which are by no means mutually exclusive). I will begin by summarising the main issues raised and discussed in each chapter.

Chapter 2 covered the role of language input (in its various conceptions) and language development. Language input was regarded as related to language development, influencing the form and the content of the language learned in the broadest possible sense. So children in the UK acquire grammatical English, those in Italy, grammatical Italian and children in Japan, grammatical Japanese. Children acquire the dominant language to which they are exposed. The specific role that the language input can play on the development of language depends very much on what is regarded as the important component—the adult providing the spoken language, the child as recipient, or the language itself. Research over the years, as was described, has focused on different aspects. Thus, the claimed magnitude and the causal force of the language input has depended on the target of the research enterprise. Not only has the focal point shifted over the years, but the nature of the influence considered important has altered. Early studies examined how adult input language influenced the *form* (i.e. the grammatical structure) of children's subsequent language. Later studies have concentrated on the impact on the *use* of language by children, the meanings intended and the conveyance of these in social and communicative interchanges.

In the 1990s, it is acknowledged that maternal speech is a facilitatory mechanism for the development of language in the child. The precise means by which this assistance is achieved is still probably underspecified and may involve multiple determinants. These could include the close form-to-function mapping imposed on maternal speech during a child's early developmental life (Ninio & Snow, 1988), the particular uses of language and the contexts of its use, with all the attendant exaggeration, repetition and ritual, or even the developmental (physiological, neurological, cognitive) status of the child himself. All aspects in their own way facilitate language development via the promotion and enhancement of social interaction. Chapter 2 focused on the first two aspects, whereas in Chapter 3, some of the prerequisites for social interaction that are apparent at birth and become refined in early infancy were considered, alongside some of the more theoretical constructs that have been proposed to account for the effectiveness of social interaction. Sensory and cognitive precursors facilitate not only language development but also predispose infants to interact socially from birth. Therefore, Chapter 3 considered those aspects of social assistance, either external or internal, that aid this process.

Although language development was adopted as the developmental ability to be attained, the conclusions from Chapter 3 are applicable to other cognitive domains. It was surmised that both external and internal assistance, provided by empathic and helpful adult assistance and by innate predispositions respectively, greatly benefit a child's linguistic development. Adult assistance supports a child's linguistic endeavours through the provision of a carefully tuned scaffold. This scaffold responds appropriately, gently easing the child into suitable language use, guiding, cajoling and directing the child towards "correct"—i.e. culturally acceptable—language forms and functions. Internal facilitatory mechanisms include well developed audition and speech perception abilities, rudimentary but functional sensory capabilities permitting interaction socially from birth, and a certain degree of harmony and co-ordination with aspects of the human voice and responsiveness to human activities.

In Chapter 4, the emphasis shifted to children's cognitive development. In so doing, priority was given to experimental studies of pre-school and school-aged children's cognitive capabilities. The theoretical orientations governing such research are different to those dealing exclusively with language, although often language is incorporated into them. The experimental studies whereby children, often in twos or threes, are exposed to different solutions to a cognitive problem led to consideration of the necessary (but probably not sufficient) social interaction conditions that facilitate development. Socio-cognitive conflict was proposed as an important impetus for cognitive change and development. Additional areas of research covered in this chapter included the research where social interaction is the context for cognitive problem solving and where it may, either inadvertently or by design, assist or hinder cognitive development.

Attention was then turned in Chapter 4 to Vygotsky's zone of proximal development and its use as a theoretical construct in research on cognitive development. Rather than conflict being postulated as a powerful interaction mechanism for growth, collaboration between peers or between an adult and a child is regarded as the causal mechanism. This research therefore dovetails with the studies that evolved from the metaphor of a scaffold. In both cases, assistance, as provided through social interaction, acts as the impetus to and the support for intellectual development (including all aspects of cognitive development and language development).

Chapter 5 then discussed two avenues that seem fruitful: *conflict* as generated by opposing perspectives (visual, spatial, cognitive) and operationalised as disagreement and *communication* between participants, in particular, conflictual but responsive talk. Both assist cognitive growth. Following on from Piaget's theory, conflict (typically as engineered by the experimenter) is regarded as the process by which cognition develops. However, more recent studies consider the interaction (sometimes characterised as collaborative) and the inherent communication as the process in which conflict (and agreement) can occur. This issue was discussed in relation to some illustrative studies.

In studies influenced directly by Vygotsky's theory, two different means by which the interaction processes assist in development can be detected and these relate to the form and the content of the interaction itself. According to Wertsch, who is closely aligned with Vygotsky's theory in its purest form, the interaction processes are themselves the solution to the cognitive tasks. Thus, in the jigsaw tasks, the strategic behaviours used by the mothers and taken over by the children within a single interaction session are the means to solve the jigsaw puzzle. Therefore, these behavioural solutions do not really facilitate problem solving *per se*; rather, they permit the solving of a specific task. Their general applicability is limited to similar tasks, and knowledge of these strategies is facilitatory in such circumstances. On the other hand, if, as is the case in the studies by Forman and Cazden (1985) and Garton and Renshaw (1988), the form of the interaction—namely, conflict, collaboration and so on—is not synonymous with its content, then the social processes of the interaction are merely a means to an end. This would also be true of the studies where communication (be it agreeable or disagreeable, cooperative or conflictual) is considered to be the important, possibly causal, aspect of the interaction.

If then, the processes inherent in social interaction, especially adult–child or child–child interaction in any cognitive or linguistic domain, are the means to the end (the solution of the problem), are these processes incorporated into any knowledge that may arise out of the interaction? The answer to this is surely "Yes". Not only do the children achieve success on the task (although this could be judged to be a by-product), but also social processes that facilitate the accomplishment of the goal are learned. For example, children learn to divide up the task into sub-goals or into tasks that one of them alone can achieve, they come to appreciate different perspectives and different points of view *en route* to solving the task, they learn how to communicate, to discuss, to describe and explain, to monitor and guide (both verbally and behaviourally), and to participate in social interaction.

Social interaction provides ample opportunity for children to learn to become skilled communicators, right from birth, through early language development to the solving of more complex cognitive problems. Social interaction allows for communication, for the evolution of a shared perspective (sometimes focused on a specific task or issue), and it encapsulates the notion of "obuchenie", the coalescence of development, learning and instruction. How then does social interaction realise this achievement? What are the processes that cause, promote, facilitate or mediate development?

MEDIATORS IN DEVELOPMENT

In order to account for the social facilitation of both language and cognition, it is crucial to identify common mediating mechanisms. The prime mediating mechanism (to describe it as causal is perhaps too strong) is, in my opinion, communication. In particular, language (or perhaps an equivalent communication system) greatly enhances one's participation in social interchanges and in society at large. It permits one to make a contribution to social interaction. From social origins develops language which then permits greater and more flexible participation in further social interactions. Language as communication also facilitates cognitive development and enables successful problem solving especially in conjunction with other people.

Whilst neither totally ignoring nor acknowledging the role of language, Azmitia and Perlmutter (1989) speculate that social input leads to learning depending on the skill of the social partner relative to the individual child. With an increase in age or a reduction in task difficulty, there is an increase in the level of performance. There is thus a hypothesised progression of social influence as a function of the child's skill level (as measured by age and/or task difficulty) and type of social input (see Fig. 6.1).

At the first level of social influence, the responsible mechanisms are most similar to those proposed by the social learning theorists. *Uninvolved* performance is characteristic of preschool children working alone. Social input in the form of motivation rather than instruction ensures the child is *engaged* in the task. At Level 2, the social mechanisms are similar to those proposed by Piaget where a conflict of perspectives is most efficacious and as a result of the social input, the child becomes *effective* at performing the task. At Level 3, Vygotsky's theory can best account for the relevant social mechanisms whereby the social input yields *efficient* task performance by the child. At Level 4, the final level, the social mechanisms characteristic of pedagogical practice are the ones most likely to affect performance. Expert input ensures improved performance, assuming a certain level of task proficiency has been achieved. *Generalisation* of skills is a measure of successful performance.

While this model is comprehensive and assimilates a range of different theoretical perspectives, it fails to take into account the communicative nature of the interactions. Another way of synthesising the opposing theoretical perspectives is to propose an interaction continuum, within which communicative processes occur, and the content of these verbal (and sometimes non-verbal) communicative interchanges can take the form of conflict, disagreement, dissent or debate, of approval, of compliance, of agreement, of the regulation and monitoring of behaviour, or of discussion, negotiation and resolution. Providing the opportunity for such interactions to take place and charting their efficacy in terms of subsequent task performance (including the adoption of strategies, the shift from other- to self- regulation and successful achievement of the goal) should be our research focus.

Before finalising this argument, let me return to Vygotsky, or more accurately, Wertsch's (1985a) interpretation of Vygotsky. Language is regarded as a powerful mediating mechanism in the development of thought. From social speech, inner, self-regulatory speech emerges around, apparently, the age of seven years. To state this in a slightly different way, at this age there emerges the ability to represent relationships mentally, and to use this new knowledge for planning and

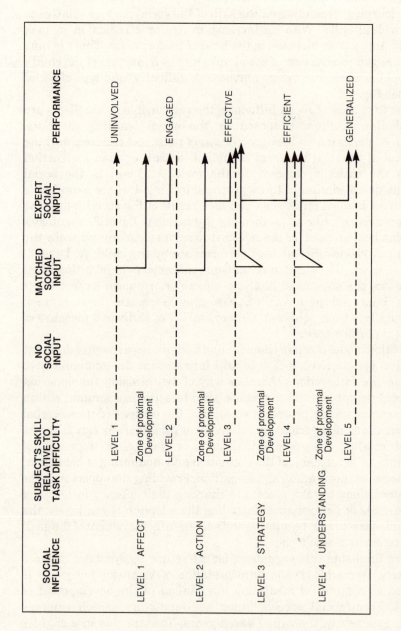

FIG. 6.1 Developmental progression of social influence on learning (Azmitzia and Perlmutter, 1989).

for monitoring one's own behaviour. The age postulated corresponds approximately to the upper level in the acquisition model of theory of mind (two to six years of age). A theory of mind involves children recognising that they themselves and others are "things which think" (Olson, Astington & Harris, 1988). It also signals an awareness of the distinction between reality and internal mental representations. Evidence for a theory of mind in children is growing (Wellman, 1990; Perner, 1991; Whiten, 1991) and it has been acknowledged that possession of a theory of mind impacts on a child's understanding of and ascription of mental states in others.

Wertsch (1985a) claims that internal representation of objects is a necessary consequence of social speech and social interaction. Representation is thus a necessary part or outcome of linguistically mediated social interaction, since cognitive objects are introduced via speech in a social context. Wertsch's research studies nearly all involve mother–child interaction, where the mother, the more experienced and competent participant, provides the linguistic mediation. Other studies by Wertsch and colleagues of teacher–child interaction or of child–child interaction always use explicit *teaching* contexts, where one participant teaches, often via language, the other. The interactional processes are the means to the end, although a satisfactory outcome is achieved. It is claimed that the socialising practices of adults—which are probably culture-specific (Wertsch, 1985a)—impart to children a certain way of talking about and then thinking about language and action. This assertion is similar to notions of theory of mind being simply part of folk psychology, a language game (Olson, 1988), as opposed to an innately determined capacity.

Garton and Pratt (1989) argue that social interaction, together with metalinguistic awareness, is a powerful mediator in the child's acquisition of language, both spoken and written. In early social interaction (even those interchanges that take place prelinguistically), cultural meanings and the significance of actions are learned. The child's own primitive communicative attempts such as head turning and crying behaviours are interpreted intentionally. Once language becomes established, the interactive interpretive system is well developed and the child knows and understands what to expect. The interpretation provided by the supportive adult in interaction is based on the cultural standards and conventions into which the child is being socialised. Thus, social processes permit the ascription of meaning to a child's developing language system, the meanings reflecting cultural conventions.

It was also argued by Garton and Pratt (1989) that the child's active role is an essential part of such a process. Children interpret what is going on around them in the world and begin to form mental representations of actions and events. An increasing awareness of these internal representations and the ability to think about processes, causes and effects, allows greater flexibility in thought and action as the child develops. In terms of both cognitive and linguistic development, children use their existing, culturally conventionalised, interpretations of the world to assist in the subsequent understanding of new actions and events and also to enable greater foresight, more efficient strategic planning and monitoring behaviours and increased understanding of the mental processes of themselves and others.

There are therefore implications for the study of the processes and mediators of social interaction that facilitate cognitive and linguistic development. The focus of research should now lie in children's understanding of the relationship not just between the participants in social interaction but between the *minds* engaged in social interaction. An additional facilitatory mechanism, I therefore would hypothesise, is *metarepresentation*, by which I mean the representation of states of knowledge or ignorance. Metarepresentational mediators would facilitate language and cognitive development through an awareness of what is known and what is not known, and how states of knowledge and ignorance can be changed and developed through social interaction.

Perner (1988) discusses the importance of what he terms higher-order mental states for the social interaction. By higher-order mental states, he refers to the fact that we, and others, are able to think, know, pretend, deceive, joke, and so on. According to research by Perner, such an understanding develops in early childhood, around the ages of three or four years. He argues that if social interaction is based on higher-order mental states (the awareness that the other participant may be thinking, joking, deceiving), then children's growing ability to understand social interaction should be related to their ability to impute or attribute higher-order mental states to others. In a series of studies conducted by Perner and his colleagues, reported in Perner (1988), young children were presented with stories in which the main character's beliefs or intentions were manipulated. By using certain social concepts such as knowledge or ignorance, lying and joking in the scenarios, it was possible to gain some insight into how children regard these social situations and how they understand and misunderstand the concepts involved. Perner concludes that an understanding of social interaction is thus based on an understanding of the mental states of the actors, or participants.

While I believe what Perner (1988) is proposing is essentially correct, namely that social interaction and the ability to attribute mental states to themselves and others by children are related, there is still a missing step in his argument. I would claim that because social interaction is so fundamental a process for the development of language and cognition, it must also be the vehicle for the transmission of culturally appropriate interpretations and representations of thinking, knowing, pretending, deceiving and so on. Perner focuses on the child's developing understanding of social interaction, neglecting the important part played by social interaction in providing graded and interpretive support for such understandings to be nurtured.

To integrate the research on language development and cognitive development, I would argue, requires an acknowledgement that a supportive social environment, with at least two active participants, is a basic prerequisite. The processes of such interaction are the key to an understanding of the mechanisms that facilitate development. Social interaction is of necessity a meeting of minds, a context wherein children learn not just the language of their community but the conventional meanings associated with actions and events. How these are transmitted varies according to the learning requirements of the child. The mother, or supportive peer or adult, assesses the child's existing state of knowledge or ignorance, and grades her expectations accordingly. A supportive scaffold thus acts as interpreter, translator and teacher for the developing child, based on an assessment of the abilities or lack of ability of the child. In addition, the scaffolder needs to take into account the goals of the interaction, whether implicit (such as in early prelinguistic exchanges) or explicit (for example, when mothers teach their children to construct a building from Lego or to solve a problem).

Similar processes take place in any interaction, between children or between adults, regardless of the specific content. The goal of the interaction needs to be established, states of knowledge and ignorance have to be ascertained, through whatever means, a mutually acceptable common ground negotiated (or imposed) before the interaction can proceed. Children's understanding of the procedural aspects of social interaction develops early on in life; what is also developing is an understanding of the cultural and social benefits of engaging in interaction with a supportive interpreter and instructor.

In order to solve any problem (linguistic or cognitive, at whatever level), children need to communicate their knowledge states to one another. They need to convey to the other participant the extent of their knowledge or their ignorance. Further, they need to convey the extent of their knowledge of the other person's knowledge or ignorance. Social interaction involving dyads of peers would probably facilitate this process. Instructional dyads (including those that facilitate language development even though the didactic element is implicit) would not facilitate this process to such an extent, since the participants are working within the zone of proximal development with one participant of necessity having greater knowledge in order to teach the other. The different knowledge states still have to be conveyed somehow, or presumed in the case of mothers talking to their young children and scaffolding the children's talk. The overriding characteristic of facilitatory cognitive and linguistic interactions is the explicitly stated or implicit differential knowledge states of the participants and the communication of these.

An example of the taking into account of differential knowledge states during communicative interaction can be seen in studies of the articles, "the" and "a" (Garton, 1983b, 1984). Correct use of the definite and indefinite articles by adult speakers (of English, at least) requires an often implicit assessment of the knowledge state of the other person. Use of the definite article assumes the referent is specific or unique to both the speaker and the listener. The indefinite article assumes a referent that is non-specific for the listener but which may be specific or non-specific for the speaker (Garton, 1984). "The", therefore, is used when the speaker assumes or knows through implicit or explicit means, such as prior specification or contextual uniqueness, that the listener knows the referent. "A", on the other hand, is used to make a referent contextually salient through naming or identifying it ("There's a man with a large hat") or it is used to refer to any one of a class of referents ("Please pass me a pencil"). In the former case, subsequent reference can then be made with the definite article since both speaker and listener have a uniquely defined "man" to refer to ("The man's hat is blue").

Young children, starting from around age two or three years, frequently use the incorrect article in their speech, leading to misidentification, communication failure and clarification requests (e.g. "Which bird?", after a child says "Look at the bird" when there are dozens flying around). Such errors may reflect the child's developing functional article system (Garton, 1983b, 1984) or may occur because young children are unaware of the potentially differential knowledge state of the other person. It is not until children are aged around nine years that they can use the articles in an adult manner, taking into account linguistic, social and contextual factors (Garton, 1984). Communication invariably involves the use of these small, common words. Their correct usage demands high levels of awareness by both participants of differential knowledge states of those engaged in social conversational interaction.

Communication also embodies the notions of instruction, learning and development as these are dependent on social interaction and the linguistic and non-linguistic processes therein. The mediating processes in social interaction that facilitate development are largely linguistic. Language permits instruction, promotes learning and facilitates development through an expressed sharing of perspectives. A shared perspective requires the transmission by each social participant of their role in the interaction, their contribution to the interaction and the means available to achieve the goal of the interaction. These may be expressed overtly, as is the case when two children are required to solve a problem together, or may be implied, as in the case of the assistance provided by mothers to their children learning language.

NEW RESEARCH EXTENSIONS OF SOCIAL INTERACTION AND LEARNING

There are a few recent research-related avenues of social interaction and learning in the applied domain, e.g. writing (Chambers, 1990) and mathematics (Lindow, Wilkinson & Peterson, 1985). I wish to focus my discussion on two: reading (Clay & Cazden, 1989) and computer-based learning (Blaye, Light, Joiner & Sheldon, 1989; Light & Blaye, 1990). The emphasis in each is on processes of dyadic interaction in applied educational contexts. The ultimate theoretical base may be different in each case, but the feasibility of adopting a perspective that holds social interaction to be a powerful facilitatory mechanism for development can be clearly seen in both. Social interaction has been demonstrated to be essential to learning, or the growth of knowledge, and extensions of research into applied areas emphasise the importance of taking the social context, and all it implies, into account.

Clay and Cazden (1989) attempt what they term a "Vygotskian" interpretation of Reading Recovery, a reading tutorial programme devised, implemented and evaluated by Clay. Reading Recovery requires that a teacher and a child collaborate in shared tasks related to reading and writing. Enhancement of reading skills, as measured by subsequent progress in reading ability, is the successful outcome of the programme. Clay and Cazden believe that Vygotsky's theory offers much by way of explanatory power for the success achieved by Reading Recovery. Collaboration between the tutor and the child on a range of literacy tasks such as shared story-book reading and writing a story facilitates the growth of reading in the child. This is accomplished by the shift from interindividual functioning to a point where the child can monitor his own reading and writing (as evidenced, for example, in self-correction during reading). The social interactional context provides a supportive environment wherein the child can develop cognitively. Like other problem-solving tasks, learning to read requires the more experienced participant, the more efficient reader, in the interaction to impart her knowledge to the less adept reader, both in terms of the strategies used to achieve reading competence and in terms of the progress made in reading.

There is a number of identifiable features of the Reading Recovery programme that ensure its success. The interaction sequence is a form of scaffolded instruction in which the teacher provides assistance to the child learner. The interaction is structured and is dominated by dialogue. Thus, there is a shared task perspective (generated by the specific reading or writing task being undertaken) and there is a particular problem to solve. The goal is the attainment of reading but success can be measured at every step, for each task or sub-task. There is a shift of responsibility for reading from the supportive adult to the child who becomes a "self-improving system". While Clay and Cazden find Vygotsky's theory and the zone of proximal development in particular a useful framework in which to interpret their work, there are other aspects of the social interaction that also engender reading improvement. Clay and Cazden themselves point to the changing forms of mediation as the teaching progresses together with the emergence of an awareness of mental processes. They also discuss the diagnosis of reading difficulties within the zone of proximal development, although they steer away from notions of learning disability.

However, the other aspect I consider important, namely the interface between instruction, learning and development ("obuchenie"), plays a leading role in the Reading Recovery programme. In many ways, this structured reading programme highlights precisely the strongpoints of social interaction theory as it encapsulates *all* the relevant components. Reading Recovery is a problem-solving situation with a clearly defined goal and can be dismantled into strategic behaviours and successful (or desirable) outcomes. The success of Reading Recovery is legendary, and it is because the programme is carefully designed to maximise the social interaction, to encourage a shared task perspective, to permit communication and dialogue, and to enable the instructional process to operate in a structured interchange. No wonder learning occurs.

The research by Light and his colleagues (e.g. Blaye et al., 1989; Light & Blaye, 1990) has adopted the theoretical position articulated by Doise and Mugny (1984). Light is now focusing his research efforts on child–child interaction and learning during computer-based problem solving. According to Light and co-workers, there are several social or interactive dimensions to be considered when examining computer-based learning. Not only is there the potential for child–child interaction during the problem-solving process, itself known to be facilitatory, but there is human–computer interaction. In addition, in the design of increasingly complex computer networks, there is the opportunity for multiple use of a system. Interaction between users, either socially or via a computer network, could well alter the learning experiences and hence the outcomes. At school, children frequently have to work in pairs or small groups due to restricted equipment or time, so any research that can show superior learning under social circumstances would certainly please those responsible for resource allocation.

Light and Blaye (1990) summarise many of the pertinent issues related to empirical studies of computer use in classrooms—issues such as type of equipment (e.g. keyboard vs. mouse operation), type of software (is it geared specifically to the computer, e.g. programming, or is it simply traditional activities transferred such as "drill-and-practice" software?) and other practicalities such as the timetabling of computer time. Experimental studies examining dyads and small groups of children as they work on a computer have yielded a range of results, due, not unexpectedly, to some of the features described above. Studies of computer problem solving have also produced ambiguous results with the effectiveness of peer interaction varying from experiment to experiment. Socio-cognitive conflict, it is hypothesised, is inadequate to account for the processes of interaction that occur in computer-based problem solving. Light and Blaye find some hope in research that is designing more "helpful" software for children plus the development of computer tasks that can act as a "partner" in the interaction and the learning process. There is a need to integrate research on peer interaction and software design. None the less, they believe that until we know more about the interactive processes that are conducive to maximise learning, it is difficult to be more precise about the social dimensions of computer-based learning.

CONCLUSIONS

The main conclusions that I wish to draw from this consideration of the influence of social interaction on both cognitive and linguistic development are best summarised in the words *communication, instruction (teaching/learning), shared perspectives* and *intentionality*. While the first three have been discussed at length, the notion of intentionality has only been discussed briefly. For many, the intentionality of the child (to communicate, to engage in social interaction, or whatever) is a central concern. Derived from Grice's (1975) conversational maxims of Quantity ("be brief"), Quality ("be truthful"), Relevance ("be relevant") and Manner ("avoid ambiguity"), Siegal (1991) has constructed a model of children's cognitive and language development. A developing understanding of these conversational rules is paralleled by advances in cognition in a range of areas. An understanding and good deployment of conversational skills is, according to Siegal, necessary for the construction of the experimenter's intent by children in the sorts of experiments commonly used to tap developing knowledge. Inexperience in constructing models of intent may mislead adults into tapping only a small part of a child's understanding. Siegal cautions that this is a very serious state of affairs, leading us to conclude that young children are deficient conceptually when in fact they have misconstrued or misinterpreted the nature and purpose of the task as communicated by the experimenter.

The study of the centrality of intentionality and communication is important and finds support from such diverse researchers as Trevarthen (1977) and Perner (1988). Whether or not the developing child, from infancy, is capable of manifesting intent has been one area of research. Adults who attribute meaning to infants' early attempts at communicative interchange sometimes claim the infant is expressing an intent. More often than not, I would counter, the adult sees cultural or social relevance in the child's behaviour (for example, early smiling— what does it mean?) and interprets it accordingly. Appropriate and conventional social responses are then exchanged (the adult smiles back).

The particular processes involved in social interaction responsible for encouraging, facilitating and supporting cognitive and linguistic development vary depending on the specific purpose of the exchange (both real and perceived) and on other more tangible aspects of the interaction (Azmitia & Perlmutter, 1989). In all cases communication between participants is essential. Communication is the fundamental process of interactive social interchanges. Communication encompasses notions of conflict and collaboration, of negotiation, of agreement and disagreement, of information exchange, of interpretation and translation, of social pleasantries and intimacies, of debate and of instruction. Instruction itself is broadly conceived as involving both teaching and learning (best encapsulated in the Russian "obuchenie", Wertsch, 1984), emphasising its interactive nature and the involvement of both teacher and learner (however defined). The establishment of a shared perspective (visual, spatial, cognitive, linguistic or conceptual), through negotiation and the ascertainment of limits or extents of knowledge of the participants, is part of the process of social interaction. Social interaction *is* fundamental to the development of language and cognition, permitting the establishment of a partnership within which communication takes place. Communication is the facilitatory mediating mechanism in the development of both language and cognition. Without it we would be unable to learn, to understand, to know or to talk; nor would we be able to engage in or contribute to social interaction itself.

References

Ames, G.J. & Murray, F.B. (1982). When two wrongs make a right: Promoting cognitive change by social conflict. *Developmental Psychology, 18,* 894-897.

Asch, S.E. (1956). Studies of independence and conformity. A minority of one against a unanimous majority. *Psychological Monographs, 70* (9).

Aslin, R.N., Pisoni, D.B., & Jusczyk, P.W. (1983). Auditory development and speech perception in infancy. In P.H. Mussen (Ed.), *Handbook of child psychology* (4th ed.), Vol. 1, M. Haith & J.J. Campos (Eds.), *Infancy and developmental psychopathology.* New York: Wiley.

Atkinson, M. (1987). Mechanisms for language acquisition: Learning, parameter-setting and triggering. *First Language, 7,* 3-30.

Azmitia, M. (1988). Peer interaction and problem solving: When are two heads better than one? *Child Development, 59,* 87-96.

Azmitia, M. & Perlmutter, M. (1989). Social influences on children's cognition: State of the art and future directions. In H.W. Reese (Ed.), *Advances in child development and behaviour,* Vol. 22. New York: Academic Press.

Baker, N.D. & Nelson, K.E. (1984). Recasting and related conversational techniques for triggering syntactic advances by young children. *First Language, 5,* 3-22.

Bates, E., Bretherton, I., Beeghly-Smith, M., & McNew, S. (1983). The social basis of language development: A reassessment. In H. Reese & L. Lipsett (Eds.), *Advances in child development.* New York: Academic Press.

Bearison, D. (1982). New directions in studies of social interaction and cognitive growth. In F. Serafica (Ed.), *Social cognitive development in context.* London: Methuen.

Bearison, D., Magzamen, S., & Filardo, E.K. (1986). Socio-cognitive conflict and cognitive growth in young children. *Merrill-Palmer Quarterly, 32,* 51-72.

Berko-Gleason, J. (1985). Studying language development. In J. Berko-Gleason (Ed.), *The development of language*. Columbus, OH: Charles Merrill Publishing Co.

Bialystok, E. (1992). Metalinguistic awareness: The development of children's representation of language. In C. Pratt & A.F. Garton (Eds.), *The development and use of systems of representation by children*. Chichester: Wiley.

Blaye, A., Light, P., Joiner, R., & Sheldon, S. (1989). *Joint planning and problem solving on a computer-based task*. The Open University Centre for Human Development and Learning, Occasional Paper.

Bohannon, J.N. & Warren-Leubecker, A. (1985). Theoretical approaches to language acquisition. In J. Berko-Gleason (Ed.), *The development of language*. Columbus, OH: Charles Merrill Publishing Co.

Borer, H. & Wexler, K. (1987). The maturation of syntax. In T. Roeper & E. Williams (Eds.), *Parameter Setting*. Dordrecht: D. Reidel Publishing Company.

Bornstein, M.H. & Bruner, J.S. (Eds.) (1989). *Interaction in human development*. Hillsdale, NJ: Lawrence Erlbaum Associates Inc.

Botvin, G.J. & Murray, F.B. (1975). The efficacy of peer modeling and social conflict in the acquisition of conservation. *Child Development, 46,* 796-799.

Bowerman, M. (1977). The acquisition of word meaning: An investigation of some current conflicts. In P.N. Johnson-Laird & P.C. Wason (Eds.), *Thinking: Readings in cognitive science*. Cambridge: Cambridge University Press.

Bowlby, J. (1969). *Attachment and loss, Vol.1, Attachment*. London: Hogarth Press.

Bowlby, J. (1977). The making and breaking of affectional bonds (I and II). *British Journal of Psychiatry, 130,* 201-210 and 421-431.

Braine, M.D.S. & Hardy, J.A. (1982). On what case categories there are, why they are and how they develop. In E. Wanner & L. Gleitman (Eds.), *Language acquisition: The state of the art*. Cambridge: Cambridge University Press.

Bremner, J.G. (1988). *Infancy*. Oxford: Basil Blackwell.

Bretherton, I. (1985). Attachment theory: retrospect and prospect. In I. Bretherton & E. Waters (Eds.), *Growing points of attachment theory and research. Monographs of the Society for Research in Child Development, 50,* Nos 1-2.

Bronfenbrenner, U. (1973). A theoretical perspective for research on human development. In H.P. Dreitzel (Ed.), *Childhood and socialisation*. London: Collier Macmillan.

Bronfenbrenner, U. (1979). *The ecology of human development*. Cambridge, Mass.: Harvard University Press.

Brown, A.L. (1978). Knowing when, where and how to remember: A problem of metacognition. In R. Glaser (Ed.), *Advances in instructional psychology,* Vol. 1. Hillsdale, NJ: Lawrence Erlbaum Associates Inc.

Brown, A.L. & Reeve, R. (1987). Bandwidths of competence: The role of supportive contexts in learning and development. In L.S. Liben (Ed.), *Development or learning: Conflict or congruence?* Hillsdale, NJ: Lawrence Erlbaum Associates Inc.

Brown, R. (1958). How shall a thing be called? *Psychological Review, 65,* 14-21.

Brown, R. (1970). *Social psychology*. London: Collier-Macmillan.

Brown, R. & Hanlon, C. (1970). Derivational complexity and the order of acquisition in child speech. In J.R. Hayes (Ed.), *Cognition and the development of language*. New York: Wiley.

Bruner, J.S. (1977). Early social interaction and language development. In H.R. Schaffer (Ed.), *Studies in mother–child interaction*. London: Academic Press.

Bruner, J.S. (1983). *Child's talk: Learning to use language.* New York: Norton.

Bruner, J.S. (1984). Vygotsky's zone of proximal development: The hidden agenda. In B. Rogoff & J.V. Wertsch (Eds.), *Children's learning in the "zone of proximal development".* San Francisco: Jossey Bass.

Bryant, P.E. (1982). The role of conflict and of agreement between intellectual strategies in children's ideas about measurement. *British Journal of Psychology, 73,* 243-351.

Bryant, P.E. & Trabasso, T. (1971). Transitive inferences and memory in young children. *Nature, 232,* 456-458.

Carey, S. (1978). The child as word learner. In M. Halle, J. Bresnan, & G.A. Miller (Eds.), *Linguistic theory and psychological reality.* Cambridge, Mass.: MIT Press.

Carey, S. (1982). Semantic development: The state of the art. In E. Wanner & L. Gleitman (Eds.), *Language acquisition: The state of the art.* Cambridge: Cambridge University Press.

Carey, S. (1985). *Conceptual change in childhood.* Cambridge, Mass.: Bradford Books/MIT Press.

Caron, A.J., Caron, R.F., & Myers, R.S. (1982). Abstraction of invariant face expressions in infancy. *Child Development, 53,* 1008-1015.

Carpenter, G.C. (1974). Mother's face and the newborn. *New Scientist, 61,* 742-744.

Cazden, C. (1965). *Environmental assistance to the child's acquisition of grammar.* Unpublished Doctoral dissertation, Harvard University.

Cazden, C. (1983). Adult assistance to language development: Scaffolds, models and direct instruction. In R.P Parker & F.A. Davis (Eds.), *Developing literacy: Young children's use of language.* Newark, Delaware: International Reading Association.

Cazden, C. (1988). Environmental assistance revisited: Variation and functional equivalence. In F. Kessel (Ed.), *The development of language and language researchers.* Hillsdale, NJ: Lawrence Erlbaum Associates Inc.

Chambers, S.M. (1990). *Agreements: The forgotten factor? The effects of prior verbal agreements on children's ideas in an essay task.* Paper presented at the 25th Annual Conference of The Australian Psychological Society, Melbourne.

Chomsky, N. (1957). *Syntactic structures.* The Hague: Mouton.

Chomsky, N. (1965). *Aspects of the theory of syntax.* Cambridge, Mass.: MIT Press.

Clark, E.V. (1987). The principle of contrast: A constraint on language acquisition. In B MacWhinney (Ed.), *Mechanisms of language acquisition.* Hillsdale, NJ: Lawrence Erlbaum Associates Inc.

Clark, E.V. (1988). On the logic of contrast. *Journal of Child Language, 12,* 317-335.

Clark, E.V. (1991). Children's language. In R. Grieve & M. Hughes (Eds.), *Understanding children.* Oxford: Basil Blackwell.

Clay, M. & Cazden, C. (1989). A Vygotskian interpretation of "Reading Recovery". In L.C. Moll (Ed.), *Vygotsky and education: Instructional implications and applications of socio-historical psychology.* Cambridge: Cambridge University Press.

Cook, V.J. (1988). *Chomsky's universal grammar.* Oxford: Basil Blackwell.

Cross, T. (1977). Mothers' speech adjustments: The contribution of selected child listener variables. In N. Waterson & C. Snow (Eds.), *The development of communication.* Chichester: Wiley.

Cross, T. (1979). Mothers' speech adjustments and child language learning: Some methodological considerations. *Language Sciences, 1,* 3-25.

DeCasper, A.J. & Fifer, W. (1980). Of human bonding: Newborns prefer their mothers' voices. *Science, 208,* 1174-1176.

Dockrell, J., Campbell, R., & Neilson, I. (1980). Conservation accidents revisited. *International Journal of Behavioural Development, 3,* 423-439.

Doise, W. & Mugny, G. (1975). Recherches sociogénétiques sur la coordination d'actions interdépendantes. *Revue Suisse de Psychologie, 34,* 160-174.

Doise, W. & Mugny, G. (1984). *The social development of the intellect.* Oxford: Pergamon Press.

Doise, W., Mugny, G., & Perret-Clermont, A-N. (1975). Social interaction and the development of cognitive operations. *European Journal of Social Psychology, 5,* 367-383.

Donaldson, M. (1978). *Children's minds.* Glasgow: Fontana.

Donaldson, M. (1982). Conservation: What is the question? *British Journal of Psychology, 73,* 199-207.

Donaldson, M. (1983). Justifying conservation: Comment on Neilson et al. *Cognition, 15,* 293-295.

Donaldson, M. & Balfour, G. (1968). Less is more: A study of language comprehension. *British Journal of Psychology, 59,* 461-471.

Donaldson, M., Grieve, R., & Pratt, C. (Eds.) (1983). *Early childhood development and education.* Oxford: Basil Blackwell.

Durkin, K. (Ed.) (1986). *Language development in the school years.* London: Croom Helm.

Durkin, K., Shire, B., Riem, R., Crowther, R.D. & Rutter, D.R. (1986). The social and linguistic context of early number word use. *British Journal of Developmental Psychology, 4,* 269-288.

Fernald, A. & Kuhl, P. (1987). Acoustic determinants of infants' preference for motherese speech. *Infant Behaviour and Development, 10,* 279-293.

Flavell, J. (1978). Metacognitive development. In J.M. Scandura & C.J. Brainerd (Eds.), *Structural/process models of complex human behaviour.* Alphen aan den Rijn, The Netherlands: Sijthoof & Noordhoff.

Flavell, J. (1985). *Cognitive development* (2nd ed.). Englewood Cliffs, NJ: Prentice-Hall Inc.

Forman, E. & Cazden, C. (1985). Exploring Vygotskian perspectives in education: The cognitive value of peer interaction. In J.V. Wertsch (Ed.), *Culture, communication and cognition: Vygotskian perspectives.* Cambridge: Cambridge University Press.

Freund, L. (1990). Maternal regulation of children's problem-solving behaviour and its impact on children's performance. *Child Development, 61,* 113-126.

Furrow D. & Nelson, K. (1986). A further look at the motherese hypothesis: A reply to Gleitman, Newport and Gleitman. *Journal of Child Language, 13,* 163-176.

Furrow, D., Nelson, K., & Benedict, H. (1979). Mothers' speech to children and syntactic development: Some simple relationships. *Journal of Child Language, 6,* 423-442.

Garton, A.F. (1983a). *Children's language use in collaborative and conflict patterns of interaction.* Presented at Third International Conference, Social Psychology and Language, Bristol.

Garton, A.F. (1983b). An approach to the study of the determiners in early language development. *Journal of Psycholinguistic Research, 12,* 513-525.

Garton, A.F. (1984). Article acquisition: Theoretical and empirical issues. *Language Sciences, 6,* 81-91.

Garton, A.F. (1986). Social interaction and cognitive development: Possible causal mechanisms. *British Journal of Developmental Psychology, 4,* 269-274.

Garton, A.F. (1992). Representation in problem solving. In C. Pratt & A.F. Garton (Eds.), *The development and use of systems of representation in children.* Chichester: Wiley.

Garton, A.F. & Pratt, C. (1989). *Learning to be literate: The development of spoken and written language.* Oxford: Basil Blackwell.

Garton, A.F. & Pratt, C. (1990). Children's pragmatic judgements of direct and indirect requests. *First Language, 10,* 51-59.

Garton, A.F. & Renshaw, P.D. (1988). Linguistic processes occurring in disagreements in young children's dyadic problem solving. *British Journal of Developmental Psychology, 6,* 275-284.

Garvey, C. (1984). *Children's talk.* London: Fontana.

Gauvain, M. & Rogoff, B. (1989). Collaborative problem solving and the development of children's planning skills. *Developmental Psychology, 25,* 139-151.

Gelman, R. & Baillargeon, R. (1983). A review of some Piagetian concepts. In P.H. Mussen (Ed.), *Handbook of child psychology,* Vol. 3, J.H. Flavell & E. Markman (Eds.), *Cognitive development.* New York: Wiley.

Gelman, R. & Gallistel, C.R. (1978). *The child's understanding of number.* Cambridge, Mass: Harvard University Press.

Gelman, S.A. & Markman, E.M. (1986). Categories and induction in young children. *Cognition, 23,* 183-209.

Glachan, M. & Light, P. (1982). Peer interaction and learning: Can two wrongs make a right? In G. Butterworth & P. Light (Eds.), *Social cognition.* Brighton: Harvester Press.

Gleitman, L.R., Newport, E.L,. & Gleitman, H. (1984). The current status of the motherese hmeansypothesis. *Journal of Child Language, 11,* 43-79.

Gleitman, L.R. & Wanner, E. (1982). Language acquisition: The state of the state of the art. In E. Wanner & L.R. Gleitman (Eds.), *Language acquisition: The state of the art.* Cambridge: Cambridge University Press.

Gleitman, L.R. & Wanner, E. (1988). Current issues in language learning. In M.H. Bornstein & M.E. Lamb (Eds.), *Developmental psychology: An advanced textbook.* Hillsdale, NJ: Lawrence Erlbaum Associates Inc.

Gold, R. (1987). *The description of cognitive development: Three Piagetian themes.* Oxford: Clarendon Press.

Goldfield, B. & Snow, C.E. (1985). Individual differences in language acquisition. In J. Berko-Gleason (Ed.), *The development of language.* Columbus, OH: Charles Merrill Publishing Co.

Golinkoff, R.M. & Ames, G.J. (1979). A comparison of fathers' and mothers' speech with their young children. *Child Development, 50,* 28-32.

Gopnik, A. (1984). The acquisition of "gone" and the development of the object concept. *Journal of Child Language, 11,* 273-292.

Gopnik, A. (1988). Three types of early word: The emergence of social words, names and cognitive-relational words in the one-word stage and their relation to cognitive development. *First Language, 8,* 49-70.

Gopnik, A. & Meltzoff, A. (1984). Semantic and cognitive development in 15- to 21-month-old children. *Journal of Child Language, 11,* 495-513.

Gopnik, A. & Meltzoff, A. (1987). Language and thought in the young child: Early semantic developments and their relationship to object permanence, means–ends understanding and categorisation. In K. Nelson & A. van Kleeck (Eds.), *Children's language*, Vol. 6. Hillsdale, NJ: Lawrence Erlbaum Associates Inc.

Greenfield, P.M. (1984). *Mind and media: The effects of television, computers and video games.* London: Fontana.

Grice, H.P. (1975). Logic and conversation. In P. Cole & J.L Morgan (Eds.), *Syntax and semantics, Vol. 3: Speech acts.* New York: Academic Press.

Grieve, R. & Garton, A.F. (1981). On the young child's comparison of sets. *Journal of Experimental Child Psychology, 32,* 443-458.

Grieve, R. & Hughes, M. (Eds.) (1991). Understanding children. Oxford: Basil Blackwell.

Hargreaves, D., Molloy, C., & Pratt, A. (1982). Social factors in conservation. *British Journal of Psychology, 73,* 231-234.

Harris, P.L. (1983). Infant cognition. In P.H. Mussen (Ed.), *Handbook of child psychology*, Vol. 2, M.M. Haith & J.J. Campos (Eds.), *Infancy and developmental psychobiology.* New York: Wiley.

Harris, P.L. (1989). *Children and emotion.* Oxford: Basil Blackwell.

Hiebeck, T. & Markman, E.M. (1987). Word learning in children: An examination of fast mapping. *Child Development, 58,* 1021-1034.

Hirsh-Pasek, K., Kemler Nelson, D., Jusczyk, P.W., Cassidy, K.W., Druss, B., & Kennedy, L. (1987). Clauses are perceptual units for young children. *Cognition, 26,* 269-286.

Hirsh-Pasek, K. & Treiman, R. (1983). Doggerel: Motherese in a new context. *Journal of Child Language, 10,* 23-37.

Hirsh-Pasek, K., Treiman, R., & Schneiderman, M. (1984). Brown and Hanlon revisited: Mothers' sensitivity to ungrammatical forms. *Journal of Child Language, 11,* 81-88.

Hoff-Ginsberg, E. & Shatz, M. (1982). Linguistic input and the child's acquisition of language. *Psychological Bulletin, 92,* 3-26.

Hyams, N. (1986). *Language acquisition and the theory of parameters.* Dordrecht: D. Reidel Publishing Co.

Hyams, N. (1987). Parameters and syntactic development. In T. Roeper & E. Williams (Eds.), *Parameter setting.* Dordrecht: D. Reidel Publishing Co.

Inhelder, B., Sinclair, H., & Bovet, M. (1974). *Learning and the development of cognition.* London: Routledge & Kegan Paul.

Izard, C.E., Huebner, R., Risser, D., McGinness, G., & Dougherty, L. (1980). The young infant's ability to produce discrete emotional expressions. *Developmental Psychology, 16,* 132-140.

Jaffe, J., Stern, D., & Peery, J.C. (1973). "Conversational" coupling of gaze behaviour in prelinguistic human development. *Journal of Psycholinguistic Research, 2,* 321-329.

Jespersen, O. (1925). *Language: Its nature, development and origin.* London: Allen and Unwin.

Jones, C.P. & Adamson, L.B. (1987). Language use in mother–child and mother–child–sibling interactions. *Child Development, 58,* 356-366.

Karmiloff-Smith, A. (1984). Children's problem solving. In M.E. Lamb, A.L. Brown, & B. Rogoff (Eds.), *Advances in developmental psychology,* Vol. 3. Hillsdale, NJ: Lawrence Erlbaum Associates Inc.

Karmiloff-Smith, A. (1986a). From meta-processes to conscious repair: Evidence from children's metalinguistic and repair data. *Cognition, 23,* 95-147.

Karmiloff-Smith, A. (1986b). Some fundamental aspects of language development after five. In P. Fletcher & M. Garman (Eds.), *Language acquisition* (2nd ed.). Cambridge: Cambridge University Press.

Kemler Nelson, D., Hirsh-Pasek, K., Jusczyk P.W., & Cassidy, K.W. (1989). How the prosodic cues in motherese might assist language learning. *Journal of Child Language, 16,* 55-68.

Kohlberg, L. & Wertsch, J.V. (1987). Language and the development of thought. In L. Kohlberg, *Child psychology and childhood education: A cognitive-developmental view.* New York: Longman.

Kontos, S. & Nicholas, J.G. (1986). Independent problem solving in the development of metacognition. *Journal of Genetic Psychology, 147,* 481-495.

Lewis, C. & Gregory, S. (1987). Parents' talk to their infants: The importance of context. *First Language, 7,* 201-216.

Liberman, A.M., Harris, K.S., Hoffman, H.S., & Griffith, B.C. (1957). The discrimination of speech sounds within and across phonemic boundaries. *Journal of Experimental Psychology, 54,* 358-368.

Light, P. (1983). Social interaction and cognitive development: A review of post-Piagetian literature. In S. Meadows (Ed.), *Developing thinking.* London: Methuen.

Light, P. & Blaye, A. (1990). Computer-based learning: The social dimensions. In H. Foot, M. Morgan, & R. Shute (Eds.), *Children helping children.* Chichester: Wiley.

Light, P., Buckingham, N., & Robbins, A.H. (1979). The conservation task as an interactional setting. *British Journal of Educational Psychology, 49,* 304-310.

Light, P. & Glachan, M. (1985). Facilitation of individual problem solving through peer interaction. *Educational Psychology, 5,* 217-225.

Light, P. & Perret-Clermont, A-N. (1989). Social context effects in learning and testing. In A. Gellatly, D. Rogers, & J.A. Sloboda (Eds.), *Cognition and social worlds.* Oxford: Clarendon Press.

Lindow, J.A., Wilkinson, L.C., & Peterson, P.L. (1985). Antecedents and consequences of verbal disagreements during small group learning. *Journal of Educational Psychology, 77,* 658-667.

Lock, A. (1980). *The guided reinvention of language.* London: Academic Press.

Luque Lozano, A. (1988). *Sociocognitive conflict reviewed.* Unpublished paper.

Luria, A.R. (1976). *Cognitive development: Its cultural and social foundations.* Cambridge, Mass.: Harvard University Press.

Macfarlane, A. (1975). Olfaction and the development of social preferences in the human neonate. In *Parent–infant interaction* (CIBA Foundation Symposium 33). Amsterdam: Elsevier.

Maratsos, M.P. & Chalkley, M. (1980). The internal language of children's syntax: The ontogenesis and representation of syntactic categories. In K. Nelson (Ed.), *Children's language,* Vol.2. Hillsdale, NJ: Lawrence Erlbaum Associates Inc.

Markman, E.M. (1989). *Categorization and naming in children: Problems of induction.* Cambridge, Mass.: Bradford Books/MIT Press.

Markman, E.M., & Hutchinson, J.E. (1984). Children's sensitivity to constraints on word meaning: Taxonomic versus thematic relations. *Cognitive Psychology, 16,* 1-27.

McGarrigle, J. & Donaldson, M. (1975). Conservation accidents. *Cognition, 3,* 341-350.

McNaughton, S. & Leyland, J. (1990). The shifting focus of maternal tutoring across different difficulty levels on a problem solving task. *British Journal of Developmental Psychology, 8,* 147-155.

McNeill, D. (1966). Developmental psycholinguistics. In F. Smith & G.A. Miller (Eds.), *The genesis of language: A psycholinguistic approach.* Cambridge, Mass.: MIT Press.

McNeill, D. (1970). *The acquisition of language: The study of developmental psycholinguistics.* New York: Harper and Row.

Meltzoff, A. (1981). Imitation, intermodal co-ordination and representation in early infancy. In G.E. Butterworth (Ed.), *Infancy and epistemology.* Brighton: Harvester Press.

Meltzoff, A. (1983). Newborn infants imitate adult facial gestures. *Child development, 54,* 702-709.

Meltzoff, A. & Moore M. (1977). Imitation of facial and manual gestures by human neonates. *Science, 198,* 75-78.

Menyuk, P. (1988). *Language development: Knowledge and use.* Glenview, IL: Scott, Foresman & Company.

Merriman, W. & Bowman, L. (1989). The mutual exclusivity bias in children's word learning. *Monographs of the Society for Research in Child Development, 54,* Nos 3-4.

Miller, S.A. & Brownell, C. (1975). Peers, persuasion and Piaget: Dyadic interaction between conservers and non-conservers. *Child Development, 46,* 992-997.

Miller, S.A., Brownell, C., & Zukier, H. (1977). Cognitive certainty in children: Effects of concept, developmental level and method of assessment. *Developmental Psychology, 13,* 236-245.

Mowrer, O. (1954). The psychologist looks at language. *American Psychologist, 9,* 660-690.

Murray, F.B. (1972). Acquisition of conservation through social interaction. *Developmental Psychology, 6,* 1-6.

Murray, F.B. (1983). Learning and development through social interaction and conflict: A challenge to social learning theory. In L.S. Liben (Ed.), *Piaget and the foundations of knowledge.* Hillsdale, NJ: Lawrence Erlbaum Associates Inc.

Murray, J. (1974). Social learning and cognitive development: Modelling effects on children's understanding of conservation. *British Journal of Psychology, 65,* 151-160.

Neilson, I., Dockrell, J., & McKechnie, J. (1983). Justifying conservation: A reply to McGarrigle & Donaldson. *Cognition, 15,* 277-291.

Nelson, K. (1973). Structure and strategy in learning to talk. *Monographs of the Society for Research in Child Development, 38,* Nos 1-2.

Nelson, K.E. (1977). Facilitating children's syntax acquisition. *Developmental Psychology, 13,* 101-107.

Nelson, K.E. (1987). Some observations from the perspective of the rare event cognitive comparison theory of language acquisition. In K.E. Nelson & A. van Kleeck (Eds.), *Children's language,* Vol. 6. Hillsdale, NJ: Lawrence Erlbaum Associates Inc.

Nelson, K.E., Carskaddon, G., & Bonvillian, J. (1973). Syntax acquisition: Impact of experimental variation in adult verbal interaction with the child. *Child Development, 44,* 497-504.

Newport, E.L., Gleitman, H., & Gleitman, L.R. (1977). "Mother, I'd rather do it myself": Some effects and non-effects of maternal speech style. In C. Snow & C.A. Ferguson (Eds.), *Talking to children: Language input and acquisition.* Cambridge: Cambridge University Press.

Ninio, A. & Bruner, J.S. (1978). The achievement and antecedents of labelling. *Journal of Child Language, 5,* 1-16.

Ninio, A. & Snow, C.E. (1988). Language acquisition through language use: The functional sources of children's early utterances. In Y. Levy, I.M. Schlesinger & M.D.S. Braine (Eds.), *Categories and processes in language acquisition.* Hillsdale, NJ: Lawrence Erlbaum Associates Inc.

Nippold, M. (Ed.) (1988). *Later language development.* Boston, Mass.: College Hill Press.

Olson, D.R. (1988). On the origins of beliefs and other intentional states in children. In J. Astington, P.L. Harris, & D.R. Olson (Eds.), *Developing theories of mind.* Cambridge: Cambridge University Press.

Olson, D.R., Astington, J.W., & Harris, P.L. (1988). Introduction. In J. Astington, P.L. Harris, & D.R. Olson (Eds.), *Developing theories of mind.* Cambridge: Cambridge University Press.

Parten, M. (1932). Social participation amongst preschool children. *Journal of Abnormal and Social Psychology, 27,* 243-269.

Pea, R. (1980). The development of negation in early child language. In D.R. Olson (Ed.), *The social foundations of language and thought: Essays in honor of Jerome S Bruner.* New York: Norton.

Penner, S. (1987). Parental responses to grammatical and ungrammatical child utterances. *Child Development, 58,* 376-384.

Perner, J. (1988). Higher order beliefs and intentions in children's understanding of social interaction. In J. Astington, P.L. Harris, & D.R. Olson (Eds.), *Developing theories of mind.* Cambridge: Cambridge University Press.

Perner, J. (1991). *Understanding the representational mind.* Cambridge, Mass.: Bradford Books/MIT Press.

Perner, J., Leekam, S., & Wimmer, H. (1984). *The insincerity of conservation questions.* Paper presented at the BPS Developmental Section Annual Conference, Lancaster.

Perner, J. & Wimmer, H. (1985). "John thinks that Mary thinks that ... " Attribution of second-order beliefs by 5- to 10-year-old children. *Journal of Experimental Child Psychology, 39,* 437-471.

Perret-Clermont, A-N. (1980). *Social interaction and cognitive development in children.* London: Academic Press.

Peterson, C. & Peterson, J. (1991). Sociocognitive conflict and spatial perspective-taking in deaf children. *Journal of Applied Developmental Psychology.*

Phelps, E. & Damon, W. (1987). *Productive social interaction strategies for cognitive growth.* Paper presented in the symposium "Peer collaboration in problem solving" (Chair: E. Phelps), SRCD biennial meeting, Baltimore.

Piaget, J. (1926). *The language and thought of the child.* London: Routledge and Kegan Paul.

Piaget, J. (1932). *The moral judgement of the child.* London: Routledge and Kegan Paul.

Piaget, J. (1972). Intellectual evolution from childhood to adolescence. *Human Development, 15,* 1-12.

Pinker, S. (1986). Productivity and conservatism in language acquisition. In W. Demopoulos & A. Marras (Eds.), *Language learning and concept acquisition.* Norwood, NJ: Ablex.

Porpodas, C.D. (1987). The one-question conservation experiment reconsidered. *Journal of Child Psychology and Psychiatry, 28,* 343-349.

Pratt, C. (1985). The transition to school: A shift from development to learning. *Australian Journal of Early Childhood Education, 10,* 11-16.

Pratt, C. (1988). The child's conception of the conservation task. *British Journal of Developmental Psychology, 6,* 157-167.

Pratt, M., Bumstead, D., & Raines, N. (1976). Attendant staff speech to the institutionalised retarded: Language use as a measure of the quality of care. *Journal of Child Psychology and Psychiatry, 17,* 133-144.

Premack, D.& Woodruff, G. (1978). Does the chimpanzee have a theory of mind? *Behavioural and Brain Sciences, 1,* 515-526

Renshaw, P.D. & Garton, A.F. (1984). The social contexts of children's acquisition of problem solving skills. In *Research and educational futures: Technology, development and educational futures, collected papers Vol. 2.* Perth: Research Branch.

Renshaw, P.D. & Garton, A.F. (1986). Children's collaboration and conflict in dyadic problem solving. In C. Pratt, A.F. Garton, W.E. Tunmer, & A.R. Nesdale (Eds.), *Research issues in child development.* Sydney: Allen & Unwin Australia.

Rice, M.L. (1990). Preschoolers' QUIL: Quick incidental learning of words. In G. Conti-Ramsden & C. Snow (Eds.), *Children's language,* Vol. 7. Hillsdale, NJ: Lawrence Erlbaum Associates Inc.

Rogoff, B. (1987). Specifying the development of a cognitive skill in its interactional and cultural context. Commentary on Saxe et al. *Monographs of the Society for Research in Child Development, 52,* No. 2, 153-159.

Rogoff, B. & Gardner, W. (1984). Adult guidance of cognitive development. In B. Rogoff & J. Lave (Eds.), *Everyday cognition: Its development in social context.* Cambridge, Mass.: Harvard University Press.

Roll, S. (1970). Reversibility training and stimulus desirability as factors in conservation of number. *Child Development, 38,* 425-442.

Romaine, S. (1984). *The language of children and adolescents.* Oxford: Basil Blackwell.

Rose, S. & Blank, M. (1974). The potency of context in children's cognition: An illustration through conservation. *Child Development, 45,* 499-502.

Sachs, J. (1985). Prelinguistic development. In J. Berko-Gleason (Ed.), *The development of language.* Columbus, OH: Charles Merrill Publishing Co.

Sachs, J., Brown, R., & Salerno, R. (1976). Adults' speech to children. In W. von Raffler Engler & Y. Lebrun (Eds.), *Baby talk and infant speech.* Lisse: Peter de Ridder Press.

Samuel, J. & Bryant, P.E. (1984). Asking only one question in the conservation experiment. *Journal of Child Psychology and Psychiatry, 25,* 315-318.

Saxe, G.B., Gearhart, M., & Guberman, S.R. (1984). The social organisation of early number development. In B. Rogoff & J.V. Wertsch (Eds.), *Children's learning in the "zone of proximal development".* San Francisco: Jossey Bass.

Saxe, G.B., Guberman, S.R., & Gearhart, M. (1987). Social processes in early number development. *Monographs of the Society for Research in Child Development, 52,* No. 2.

Scollon, R. & Scollon, S. (1979). *Narrative, literacy and face in interethnic communications.* Norwood, NJ: Ablex.

Shatz, M. & Gelman, R. (1973). The development of communication skills: Modifications in the speech of young children as a function of the listener. *Monographs of the Society for Research in Child Development, 38,* No. 5.

Shipley, E., Gleitman, L.R., & Smith, C. (1969). A study in the acquisition of language: Free responses to commands. *Language, 45,* 322-342.

Shultz, T.R. (1980). Development of the concept of intention. In W.A. Collins (Ed.), *Development of cognition, affect and social relations: The Minnesota symposia on child psychology,* Vol. 13. Hillsdale, NJ: Lawrence Erlbaum Associates Inc.

Siegal, M. (1991). *Knowing children: Experiments in conversation and cognition.* Hove: Lawrence Erlbaum Associates Ltd.

Silverman, I.W. & Geiringer, E. (1973). Dyadic interaction & conservation induction: A test of Piaget's equilibration model. Child Development, 44, 815-820.

Silverman, I.W. & Stone, J.M. (1972). Modifying cognitive functioning through participation in a problem-solving group. *Educational Psychology, 63,* 603-608.

Snow, C.E. (1972). Mothers' speech to children learning language. *Child Development, 43,* 549-465.

Snow, C.E. (1977). Mothers' speech research: From input to interaction. In C. Snow & C. Ferguson (Eds.), *Talking to children: Language input and acquisition.* Cambridge: Cambridge University Press.

Snow, C.E. (1984). Parent–child interaction and the development of communicative ability. In R.L. Schiefelbusch & J. Pickar (Eds.), *The acquisition of communicative competence.* Baltimore: University Park Press.

Snow, C.E. (1986). Conversations with children. In P. Fletcher & M. Garman (Eds.), *Language acquisition* (2nd ed.). Cambridge: Cambridge University Press.

Snow, C.E. (1989). Understanding social interaction and language acquisition; Sentences are not enough. In M. Bornstein & J.S. Bruner (Eds.), *Interaction in human development.* Hillsdale, NJ: Lawrence Erlbaum Associates Inc.

Snow, C.E., Arlmann-Rupp, A., Hassing, Y., Jobse, J., Joosten, J., & Vorster, J. (1976). Mothers' speech in three social classes. *Journal of Psycholinguistic Research, 5,* 424-444.

Snow, C.E., Perlmann, R., & Nathan, D. (1987). Why routines are different: Toward a multiple-factors model of the relation between input and language acquisition. In K.E. Nelson & A. van Kleeck (Eds.), *Children's language,* Vol. 6. Hillsdale, N.J.: Lawrence Erlbaum Associates Inc.

Stark, R. (1979). Prespeech segmental feature development. In P. Fletcher & M. Garman (Eds.), *Language acquisition* (1st ed.). Cambridge: Cambridge University Press.

Stark, R. (1986). Prespeech segmental feature development. In P. Fletcher & M. Garman (Eds.), *Language acquisition* (2nd ed.). Cambridge: Cambridge University Press.

Stern, D. (1974). Mother and infant at play: The dyadic interaction involving facial, vocal and gaze behaviours. In M. Lewis & L. Rosenblaum (Eds.), *The effect of the infant on its caretaker,* Vol. 1. New York: Wiley.

Stern, D., Beebe, B., Jaffe, J., & Bennett, S. (1977). The infant's stimulus world during social interaction: A study of caregiver behaviours with particular reference to repetition and timing. In H.R. Schaffer (Ed.), *Studies in mother–child interaction.* London: Academic Press.

Stern, D., Jaffe, J., Beebe, B., & Bennett, S. (1975). Vocalising in unison and in alternation: Two modes of communication within mother–infant dyads. *Annals of the New York Academy of Sciences, 263,* 89-100.

Stern, D., Spieker, S., & MacCain, K. (1982). Intonation contours as signals in maternal speech to prelinguistic infants. *Developmental Psychology, 18,* 727-735.

Sugarman, S. (1984). The development of preverbal communication: Its contribution and limits in promoting the development of language. In R.L. Schiefelbusch & J. Pickar (Eds.), *The acquisition of communicative competence.* Baltimore: University Park Press.

Taylor, M. & Gelman, S.A. (1988). Adjectives and nouns: Children's strategies for learning new words. *Child Development, 59,* 411-419.

Tizard, B. & Hughes, M. (1984). *Young children learning: Talking and thinking at home and at school.* London: Fontana.

Tomasello, M. & Todd, J. (1983). Joint attention and lexical acquisition style. *First Language, 4,* 197-211.

Trevarthen, C. (1977). Descriptive analyses of infant communicative behaviour. In H.R. Schaffer (Ed.), *Studies in mother–child interaction.* London: Academic Press.

Trevarthen, C. (1986). Development of intersubjective motor control in infants. In M. Wade & H.T.A. Whiting (Eds.), *Motor development in children.* The Hague: Martinus Nijhof.

Trevarthen, C. (1987). Motives for culture in young children: Their natural development through communication. In W.A. Koch (Ed.), *Proceedings of symposium "Nature of culture".* Ruhr-Universitat Bochum.

Tudge, J. & Rogoff, B. (1989). Peer influences on cognitive development: Piagetian and Vygotskian perspectives. In M. Bornstein & J.S. Bruner (Eds.), *Interaction in human development.* Hillsdale, NJ: Lawrence Erlbaum Associates Inc.

Vandell, D.L. & Wilson, K.S.(1987). Infants' interactions with mother, sibling and peer: Contrasts and relations between interaction systems. *Child Development, 58,* 176-186.

Vygotsky, L. (1962). *Thought and language.* Cambridge, Mass.: MIT Press.

Vygotsky, L. (1978). *Mind in society: The development of higher mental processes.* Cambridge, Mass.: Harvard University Press.

Vygotsky, L. (1986). *Thought and language* (2nd ed.). Cambridge, Mass.: MIT Press.

Wallach, L. & Sprott, R.L. (1964). Inducing number conservation in children. *Child Development, 41,* 501-507.

Wallach, L., Wall, A.J., & Anderson, L. (1967). Number conservation: The roles of reversibility, addition–subtraction and misleading perceptual cues. *Child Development, 38,* 425-442.

Warren-Leubecker, A. & Bohannon, J.N. (1982). The effects of expectation and feedback on speech to foreigners. *Journal of Psycholinguistic Research, 11*, 207-215.

Wellman, H.M. (1990). *The child's theory of mind.* Cambridge, Mass.: Bradford Books/MIT Press.

Wells, C.G. (1985a). *Language development in the preschool years.* Cambridge: Cambridge University Press.

Wells, C.G. (1985b). Preschool literacy related activities and later success in school. In D.R. Olson, N. Torrance, & A. Hildyard (Eds.), *Literacy, language and learning: The nature and consequences of reading.* Cambridge: Cambridge University Press.

Wells, C.G. (1987). *The meaning makers.* London: Hodder and Stoughton.

Wells, C.G. & Robinson, W.P. (1982). The role of adult speech in language development. In C. Fraser & K. Scherer (Eds.), *The social psychology of language.* Cambridge: Cambridge University Press.

Wertsch, J.V. (1980). *Semiotic mechanisms in joint cognitive activity.* Paper presented at joint US-USSR Conference on the Theory of Activity, Moscow.

Wertsch, J.V. (1984). The zone of proximal development: Some conceptual issues. In B. Rogoff & J.V. Wertsch (Eds.), *Children's learning in the "zone of proximal development".* San Francisco: Jossey Bass.

Wertsch, J.V. (1985a). *Vygotsky and the social formation of mind.* Cambridge, Mass.: Harvard University Press.

Wertsch, J.V. (Ed) (1985b). *Culture, communication and cognition: Vygotskian perspectives.* Cambridge: Cambridge University Press.

Wertsch, J.V. (1985c). Adult–child interaction as a source of self-regulation in children. In S.R. Yussen (Ed.), *The growth of reflection in children.* New York: Academic Press.

Wertsch, J.V., McNamee, G.D., McLane, J.B., & Budwig, N.A. (1980). The adult–child dyad as a problem-solving system. *Child Development, 51*, 1215-1221.

Wertsch, J.V., Minick, N., & Arns, F. (1984). The creation of context in joint problem solving. In B. Rogoff & J. Lave (Eds.), *Everyday cognition: Its development in social context.* Cambridge, Mass.: Harvard University Press.

Wertsch, J.V. & Rogoff, B. (1984). Editors' notes. In B. Rogoff & J.V. Wertsch (Eds.), *Children's learning in the "zone of proximal development".* San Francisco: Jossey Bass.

Wexler, K. & Culicover, P.W. (1980). *Formal principles of language acquisition.* Cambridge, Mass.: MIT Press.

Whiten, A. (Ed.) (1991). *Natural theories of mind.* Oxford: Basil Blackwell.

Wilcox, B.M. (1969). Visual preferences of human infants for representations of the human face. *Journal of Experimental Child Psychology, 7,* 10-20.

Williams, E. (1987). Introduction. In T. Roeper & E. Williams (Eds.), *Parameter setting.* Dordrecht: D. Reidel Publishing Co.

Wood, B. (1976). *Children and communication: Verbal and nonverbal language development.* Englewood Cliffs, NJ: Prentice Hall.

Wood, D. (1980). Teaching the young child: Some relationships between social interaction, language and thought. In D.R. Olson (Ed.), *The social foundations of language and thought: Essays in honor of Jerome S Bruner.* New York: Norton.

Wood, D. (1988). *How children think and learn.* Oxford: Basil Blackwell.

Wood, D. (1989). Social interaction as tutoring. In M. Bornstein & J.S. Bruner (Eds.), *Interaction in human development.* Hillsdale, NJ: Lawrence Erlbaum Associates Inc.

Wood, D., Bruner, J.S., & Ross, G. (1976). The role of tutoring in problem solving. *Journal of Child Psychology and Psychiatry, 17,* 89-100.

Author Index

Subject Index

THE DEVELOPMENT OF YOUNG CHILDREN'S SOCIAL-COGNITIVE SKILLS
MICHAEL A. FORRESTER (University of Kent)

This book presents a new theoretical framework for investigating children's social cognitive skills. Beyond being the first major review of social-cognitive literature, this synopsis articulates why contemporary theoretical ideas (e.g. information processing, Piagetian and social interactionist) are unlikely ever to provide the conceptual basis for understanding children's participative skills.

Building upon ideas both within and beyond mainstream developmental psychology, the "eco-structural" approach advocated seeks to draw together the advantages of the ecological approach in perceptual psychology with the considerable insights of the conversational analysts, child language researchers and Goffman's analysis of social interaction. This convergence is centred around the dynamic and participatory realities of engaging in conversational contexts, *the* locus for acquiring social cognitive skills.

ISBN 0-86377-232-3 March 1992 176pp. $25.50 £14.95 hbk.

ANALOGICAL REASONING IN CHILDREN
USHA GOSWAMI (University of Cambridge)

Analogical reasoning is a fundamental cognitive skill, involved in classification, learning, problem-solving and creative thinking, and should be a basic building block of cognitive development. However, for a long time researchers have believed that children are incapable of reasoning by analogy. This book argues that this is far from the case, and that analogical reasoning may be available very early in development.

ISBN 0-86377-226-9 June 1992 176pp. $26.95 £14.95 hbk.

LANGUAGE LEARNING
A Special Case for Developmental Psychology?
CHRISTINE J. HOWE (University of Strathclyde)

The starting place for this book is the notion, current in the literature for around thirty years, that children could not learn their native language without substantial innate knowledge of its grammatical structure. It is argued that the notion is as problematic for contemporary theories of development as it was for theories of the past. The book attempts an in-depth study of the notion's credibility, arguing that it runs into two major problems. Firstly, proponents of the innateness hypothesis are too ready to treat children as embryonic linguists, concerned with the representation of sentences as an end in itself. Secondly, even when the communication analogy is adopted, it is glibly assumed that the meanings children impute will be the ones adults intend. One of the book's major contentions is that a careful reading of contemporary research suggests that the meanings may differ considerably.

ISBN 0-86377-230-7 late 1992 176pp. $26.95 £14.95 hbk.

PUBLISHED BY LAWRENCE ERLBAUM ASSOCIATES
Please send orders to: Afterhurst Mail Order Department, 27 Church Road, Hove, East Sussex, BN3 2FA England Tel: (0273) 748427 Fax: (0273) 205612

LANGUAGE EXPERIENCE AND EARLY LANGUAGE DEVELOPMENT
From Input to Uptake
MARGARET HARRIS (University of London)

This book is about one of the most fundamental debates on language development, namely the relationship between children's language development and their language experience. This issue is not only of theoretical interest: understanding how a child's language development is related to experience, has important implications for children whose early language development is giving cause for concern. If there are no environmental influences on early development then little can be done to help the child whose first steps into language are faltering. But, if the speed with which children develop language is subject to some external influence, then there are likely to be opportunities for successful intervention and grounds for optimism rather than pessimism in this area. This book argues that there are grounds for optimism.

ISBN 0-86377-231-5 late 1992 176pp. $24.95 £14.95 hbk.

CHILDREN'S SAVING
Studies in the Development of Economic Behaviour
EDMUND J. S. SONUGA-BARKE (Southampton University),
PAUL WEBLEY (Exeter University)

Children, just like adults, are faced with practical problems of resource allocation. Their response to these problems may be different from those of adults but no less "economic" for that.

The authors studied the way children tackle the particular problems posed by limitations of income. How do children learn, a) the relationship between choices available in the present and the future, b) to spread their limited financial resources over time into the future and c) about the strategies, such as banking, that allow them to protect those resources from threats and temptations? In short, how do children learn to save?

This volume goes some way to answering these and related questions and in so doing sets up an alternative framework for the study of the emergence of economic awareness.

ISBN 0-86377-233-1 late 1992 176pp. $26.95 £14.95 hbk.

Other Titles in the Essays in Developmental Psychology Series
GOODNOW/COLLINS: **Development According To Parents**
ISBN 0-86377-160-2 1990 150pp. $31.95 £19.95 hbk.

ISBN 0-86377-161-0 1990 150pp. $15.95 £8.95 pbk.

GOSWAMI/BRYANT: **Phonological Skills and Learning to Read**
ISBN 0-86377-150-5 1990 160pp. $31.95 £19.95 hbk.

ISBN 0-86377-151-3 1990 160pp. $13.95 £8.95 pbk.

SIEGAL: **Knowing Children, Experiments in Conversation and Cognition**
ISBN 0-86377-158-0 1991 128pp. $31.95 £19.95 hbk.

ISBN 0-86377-159-9 1991 128pp. $15.95 £8.95 pbk.